C000133128

SOLD

BEING AN

E S S A Y

Offer'd to all of that Profession.

AUTHORIS'D

By many late Examples, especially
in the Late W A R S

BETWEEN

France and *Holland*;

Containing divers

OBSERVATIONS .

Upon several

Remarkable Accidents, which hap
pened in those W A R S.

L O N D O N,

Printed for *Benj. Tooke*, at the *Ship* in S. *Paul's*
Church-yard, and *Ja. Tonson* at the *Judges-
head* in *Chancery-lane* near *Fleet-street*. 1686.

The Naval & Military Press Ltd

published in association with

ROYAL
ARMOURIES

Published by
The Naval & Military Press Ltd
Unit 10 Ridgewood Industrial Park,
Uckfield, East Sussex,
TN22 5QE England
Tel: +44 (0) 1825 749494
Fax: +44 (0) 1825 765701
www.naval-military-press.com

in association with

ROYAL
ARMOURIES

The Naval & Military
Press

MILITARY HISTORY AT YOUR
FINGERTIPS

... a unique and expanding series of reference works

Working in collaboration with the foremost
regiments and institutions, as well as acknowledged
experts in their field, N&MP have assembled a
formidable array of titles including technologically
advanced CD-ROMs and facsimile reprints of
impossible-to-find rarities.

Printed and bound by Antony Rowe Ltd, Eastbourne

THE

CONTENTS.

CHAP. I.

THAT of all the Conditions of Life, there is none so noble for ones self, nor so useful for ones Country, as that of a Soldier. Page 1

CHAP. II.

That an Officer ought to be indued with Religion, as well for the effect

A 3

The Content.

The Contents.

CHAP.

The Contents.

CHAP.

The Contents.

CHAP. XI.

CHAP. XII.

CHAP. XIII.

CHAP.

The Contents.

Chap.

The Contents.

————————

THE

THE

SOLDIERS GUIDE.

CHAP. I.

*That of all the Conditions of Life,
there is none so noble for ones self,
nor so useful for ones Country, as
that of a Soldier.*

THERE are four Conditions in a Civil Life.
1. That of the Sword:
2. That of the Gown:
3. That of Trade: 4. That of Husbandry: These Four are all useful in a State. The Soldiers part is the making it great; repressing the Enterprises of the Enemies; and containing the People within the duty and respect which they owe

B   to

to their Sovereign. The Gown-
men, they make the Laws flourish; hinder the Stronger from op-
pressing the Weaker: and restrain
the Wicked by the fear of Punishment. The Merchants transport
into Forreign Countries what we
have of superfluous, and import
what we have not enough of. By
the means of these we have Mony
for what is superfluous, and we
have from abroad what either Necessity or Curiosity can make us
desire. The Labourers they Till
and Sow the Ground, and their
pains are as useful to the Rich as
the Poor, since they both gain by
their Labour: But although in all
these Conditions every one concurs
in advancing the good and greatness
of the State: Yet in my opinion,
of all the Conditions of Life a Man
can chuse, there is none so useful
to his Country, nor so honorable
for himself as that of a Soldier.

In

In effect if we consider the Dangers whereto he expofes himself every day; muft not we all agree, that as he facrifices all that is moft dear to him, for the fafety of his Country; I mean even to the very laft drop of his Blood? So his Country is much otherwife obliged to him, than to thofe who only afford it a few careful Days and watchful Nights. Add to this that his Country it felf could not fubfift without him, fince as I have faid, he doth not only make it his bufinefs to enlarge its Dominion but to defend it alfo againft all the attempts of its Enemies; but that which admits of no contradiction, is that 'tis he who is even the fupport of the Gown-man, the Merchant, and the Husbandman; for how fhould the Gentlemen of the Long Robe make the Laws to be obferved, if there were not a Soldiery in the State to render the

B 2 Prince

Prince powerful enough to enforce
the Wicked to submit to his Laws?
Or how would the Merchant be a-
ble to make Trade flourish, if there
were not Men of War to convoy
them into Forreign Parts, and to
guard them safely back into our
own Ports? And lastly how can
the Husbandman till his Ground,
unless the Soldier keeps him in
Peace? Let us then conclude from
what I have already said; That
of all Professions, there is none
so Noble for a Man, or so useful
to the State, as that of Men who
know the Profession of Arms.
Therefore it is not to be admired,
if those who have any ambition,
prefer it before all others. But
since this Condition requires many extraordinary Qualities to succeed well in it, I will venture to
say there is nothing so dangerous
as to enter into it without examining ones self, whether one be
pro-

proper for it. Firſt, then, as every one knows there is Courage required; and therefore I ſhall ſay nothing of it here, ſuppoſing every one will inform himſelf enough of it: But this I ſhall obſerve, that no Man can be truly brave if he does not fear God; and I muſt lay it down for a Principle, that the Quality which is moſt neceſſary for a Soldier, is to be a good Man. Secondly, this Condition requires Wiſdom; and provided he have theſe two Qualities, I will maintain there is nothing which he may not reaſonably hope for; beſides the reaſons which I ſhall alledg, to prove what I have ſaid, there are a Thouſand Examples which ought to convince, ſome of which I ſhall hereafter give, becauſe I know Examples do often make more impreſſion upon the minds of Men, than all the reaſons which can be brought; and when

I have proved these two things, I
shall pass to some Observations I
made whilst I was in Service, which
I doubt not but will be of use
to those who design to engage themselves in this Noble Profession:
For after having often observed
that those who had the most experience, could not avoid sometimes committing of Errors; with
much more reason am I induced
to believe, that those who have
had none at all, have need of some
Lessons which may hinder them
from committing them, that is to
say in common things; for I must
have been void of judgment to
pretend that a Soldier can learn
his Profession in a Book. All these
remarks are drawn from Examples
which have happened so lately,
that if there be any thing found
in them so surprizing, as to make
them doubted of, it will be easie
to clear it, there being few now in
                              Service

Service, who by refreshing their memories, will not remember whatever I here advance to be true; and to give the more Authority to what I shall say, I shall often name the Persons I speak of, unless I say something to their disadvantage, in which case I hope I may be pardoned if I abstain from doing it, my intention being not to speak evil of any body: I shall not pretend to any great order in this Book, because if I did, I might possibly find it difficult to succeed in it, Men of my Profession most commonly making better use of the Sword than of the Pen; besides, my intention is not to write a History, which would require more circumspection, but a Collection of many things, which when found useful, will always be lookt upon as well enough written.

B 4   CHAP.

CHAP. II.

That an Officer ought to be indued with Religion, as well for the effect which that produces in the Minds of others, as for the Advantage he will receive from it towards the making of his Fortune.

THere is not in being a Man so wicked, as not to believe in his heart there is a God, and who doth not fear his Judgment; all that we see in Nature instructs us there is something above us; and when we would not confess it, we feel every day so many Benefits which flow from it, that that is more than sufficient to convince us of it, in spight of our selves : There was no more required to make the Ancients confess that there was some Being above which governed all

we

we fee, they being fo fully perfwaded of this Truth, that they
commanded very rigorous Punifhments to be inflicted on thofe
who maintained the contrary op-
pinion; for *Prothagoras* one of the
firft Philofophers, was banifhed
from *Athens*, for having maintained, that every thing was produced
by Nature. And *Anaxagoras* who
followed him in his Errors, was
put in Prifon for the fame thing:
And *Socrates* condemned to death.
Then certainly ought it to be very fhameful for us, that Men who
had no other light, but that of
reafon fhould teach us what we
ought to believe: Here would be
a good place for a large Moral Difcourfe, if that were my Subject,
but it not being fo, I fhall content my felf with faying that it is
fo neceffary for an Officer to make
himfelf known to be indued with
Religion, that without it I do not

think he can hope to make his Fortune. And in my opinion there are Four convincing Reasons for it; First there cannot be any great trust reposed in a Man who forgets his Duty to God, for much more it is to be presumed that he will forget what is due from him to the King. Secondly, it is a very bad way to make himself esteemed to appear irrilegious, it being peculiar to impiety, to treat an aversion to it in all the World, even in the most debauched. The third Reason is, that he cannot be brave who is not pious; for let an ill Man counterfeit never so much, he always goes into the Battel with fear, and if it were in his own choice alone he would not go. The fourth is, that he cannot hope for any great Commands, because in the Fight the pricks and remorse of Conscience will so disturb his Mind, that he cannot bring himself off with Honour. But

But I would not be underſtood
here to blame in the leaſt that re-
morſe of Conſcience which often
works good effects;but I ſay,That if
our Religion requires us to take
another time to look to our Conſcience, the King's ſervice requires it
yet much more:An undiſturbed preſence of mind being then abſolutely
neceſſary , ſo as to know how to
make ones beſt advantage.I very well
know, that the moſt impious affect
this preſence of mind, when they
are commanded out; but notwithſtanding all their endeavours to
diſguiſe it, it is eaſie to ſee they
do not enjoy the calmneſs of mind
they affect; and when they are
engaged in Fight, it is yet much
more eaſie to perceive the diſtur-
bance and agitation wherein they
are. I deſire for Witneſſes no others
than the Perſons themſelves, who
have happened to be upon ſervice without having put in order
the.

the Affairs of their Confcience, and if they will but be fincere, I am fure they will confefs they never were fo much perplexed : But if this truth muft be authorized by Examples, many debauchees will furnifh me but with too many, of fuch who have marched into the Battel without fearing any thing, and fo much as thinking there was a God ; and yet notwithftanding, no fooner were they Wounded , but they fpoke of nothing but of his Judgments, and of the fear they were in of them : So true it is, that there is no Perfon who can forbear trembling when he thinks what an account he muft give of his Actions to the Divine Juftice. I might have had thoufands of Examples, as I have faid, to prove this truth, but I fhall content my felf with mentioning only two , the one a Captain of Dragoons furnifhes me with, and the other the Count *de Guiche,* whofe

whose Death was so different from
his Life, that we cannot enough
admire the Judgments of God,
which when he pleases produces
such great changes.

A Captain of the Dragoons of
the most Irreligious of the Army,
and who had a Vanity to be thought
so, having been dangerously wounded at the Battel of *Turkheim*,
the Chyrurgions advised him to
think of his Conscience; and se-
ing that they did in earnest despair of his Cure, he began to shed
so many Tears that they made
more shew than the Bloud he shed
out of his Wound; he said to all
those that came to see him, that
he had no fear of Death at all,
but that the Judgments of God
made him tremble; that although
he had always seemed to have no
Religion, yet the stings of Conscience had made him learn that
he was at last to give an account
of

of all his Actions; that he beg'd
their pardons for the Scandal which
he had given them, and that if it
should please God to give him time
to repent, he hoped by his change
of Life to shew what his Repentance
was: At the same time he threw
himself out of the bed upon the
ground, kissing the Earth, and asking
every one if he thought after all
the Crimes he had committed
God would be so merciful as to
pardon him? It did please God
to give him time for Repentance,
and he being restored to his health,
retired amongst the Fathers of the
Oratory, where he now lives.

The Count *de Guiche* Lieutenant
General of the King's Armies, was
a Man of extraordinary Merit and
great Learning; but had not in his
youth been free from the Extra-
vagances incident to it, (and the e-
vil Example of some Debauchees
had so much power over him, as

to

to feduce him contrary to his inclination, and the height of his own reafon) finding himfelf upon his Death-bed, he was defirous, that as all the Court had been Witneffes of his failings, they fhould alfo be fo of his repentance; he fpoke of his paft Diforders with fo deep a regret, and fo feeling an Eloquence, that they were all edified by him, making fuch a defcription of the Vanities of the Age, as they then appeared to him, that he made even thofe who were plunged the deepeft into them, fenfible that they fought nothing thereby but their own ruine and deftruction; he bad them take example by him, and reflect upon what he carried out of the World, after having poffeft fo much Honour and Riches: In a word he died with fo good thoughts, and fo worthy of a Chriftian, that none went from him without Tears in
their

their Eyes, and extreamly edified
by the Conversion of this Lord,
who had so totally resign'd himself up to the Will of God.

C H A P. III.

*That Wisdom is necessary for a Sol-
dier and that without it he cannot hope to make his Fortune.*

THis Chapter has great relation to the foregoing one;
for as the wise Man saith, *The fear
of the Lord is the beginning of Wisdom:* So I had reason to make
the fear of God to precede Wisdom, and to say that that is the
first Quality which is necessary for
a Soldier. But I am not of opinion that the Wisdom of a Soldier consists in a grave outside, which
ought on the contrary always to
be free and pleasant; for it will
be

be much better for him to be merry, than dull and sad; but I would have him shew it by digesting well a design as he should do by obviating the difficulties which may hinder its execution, and at length by executing it with Conduct. These three parts are so necessary for a Soldier to supply, that if he fails in either of the three, he cannot hope to gain any great Reputation: For what good will it do him to have formed a great design, if he knows not how to remove all obstructions to the effecting of it; or if he wants conduct in the execution of it: A Man must therefore (before he engages in this Profession) sound himself, and consider what he is proper for. For if a Man has not solid and penetrating Parts, it is in vain for him to hope to make any great Fortune; War does not consist in only knowing how to strike, but

when

when to ftrike to the purpofe ;
Many times there muft be recourfe
had to Stratagem and Invention,
for he who pretends always to
overcome his Enemy with open
force, will often run the hazard
of doing him no great hurt: one
muft know what part to act according to the occafion, fometimes
charge, and fometimes retreat:
For although fometimes rafh Actions prove lucky; yet a Man is
more to be commended for doing
what he ought, than for happening to beat the Enemy, when he
ought not to have fought. Now,
we ought not to imagin that this
prudence in thefe Actions is only
neceffary for Generals, for every
private Captain hath as much need
as they, and it happens in many
occafions that this is his only Con-
fellour and director; and if he then
fails of doing what is expected
from a wife Man, let him never
ex-

expect to be entrusted with any
other Commands, of which the
Generals will be sure to take care,
for it would shew as much want
of judgment in them as in him,
if after having known his want of
Capacity, they should intrust him
with any great Affairs.

CHAP. IV.

*That a Man must be assured of his
own Courage, before he resolves
to be a Soldier.*

SInce I have only said a word
by the by concerning the Courage which a Man ought to have
that goes into the Army; it will
not be improper to speak more
largely of it here, because many
People engage themselves without
reflection, and without consider-
ing the inconveniences which may
happen;

happen; besides I look upon it as
a general Rule, that before we im-
brace any Condition, we muft think
well of it : for it were much
better not to have undertaken a
thing, than not to acquit one felf
as one ought to do of it. This
reflection is particularly neceffary
for a Man who defigns to make
Arms his profeffion , becaufe the
accidents which may happen in it
are of much greater confequence
than in any other condition : For
example, If a Man makes himfelf
a Merchant, and does not know
his Trade, the only hazard he runs
is of lofing his Eftate , but
does not lofe his Honour : In the
fame manner, a Man who betakes
himfelf to the Gown , and who
with a moderate fufficiency of
Partts, endeavours to diftribute
Juftice to every one, tho he may
not pafs for an able Man, yet doth
at leaft for a good Judg : But a
Sol-

Soldier who suffers the least stain in his Reputation is a Man without Honour. There are always Persons who examine his conduct, and do not pardon the least thing in him; he must be stout in the greatest dangers; he must have Prudence in all Enterprizes; he must be able to penetrate into the most difficult Affairs, and be active in the execution of them; he must not suffer any indignity to be put upon him, and yet not be quarrellsom; for if he be not possest of all these Qualities, he is a Man of no consideration amongst the Men of Service, and cannot pretend to distinguish himself but to his own prejudice: Notwithstanding most Men without making reflection upon all these things, go into the War as if they went into *Hide-Park*, or to a Feast: They suffer themselves to be taken by the Eyes, and are charmed

by

by the Gold-lace they obferve upon the back of an Officer, or fome
embroidered Saddle and Hoofe
which they fee upon a fine Horfe,
they think prefently 'tis but going
into the War to have all this,
not confidering that to fupport this
finery they who have them muft
have had a great Eftate of their
own , or that the King has re-
compenced their actions with
great gifts, or which is moft to
be feared, a great many miferable
Families have been ruined for it
in a Winter Quarters. The Ladies contribute very much to en-
cline young Men to take this
refolution , becaufe they obferve
that the Soldiers are efteemed by
them above all others, there is
nothing that they will not do to
gain their favour ; but truly I think
they buy it at a little too dear a
rate, who go into the Army only out of complaifance, and without

out being ſtirred up to it by their own inclinations. I have ſeen ſome ſo weary of it even at the begining of the firſt Campaign, that it moved Compaſſion to ſee them; for notwithſtanding the toyl is great there, that ought not to be a reaſon againſt a Man's embracing this Condition, if he have the leaſt ſhare of reſolution and health, for the Bodies of Men harden themſelves infenſibly for a fatigue, and ſome who find themſelves incommoded the firſt Campaign, forget it in a years time; therefore there is in my opinion but one thing only which can diſſwade a Man of Quality from taking the Sword, that is if he finds he hath not Courage enough; for if ſo, he would do himſelf the greateſt injury in the World to go on purpoſe to ſhew his Infamy in ſo good company, there being ſo many other conditions which he may chooſe, in which he may notwithſtanding gain a Reputation,

putation. For example it would
be no shame for him not to be
thought stout if he makes himself
a Clergy-man or a Lawyer, or be of
any other Profeffion; but so soon
as he has put a Sword to his side,
he is laughed at by all the World
if he omits doing his Duty: I have
seen many expofed to fcorn and
raillery, for want of having made
this reflection; and amongft others,
a Brother of one of the chief Ma-
giftrates of *Paris*, who was a Captain of Horfe, and fled fo foon as
he perceived the Enemy, which
caufed the King to cafhier him,
and fend him home with Difhonour: whereas had he but taken
upon him a Gown, as his Brother
had done, he might have lived with
Reputation, and been efteem'd by all
the World. I have alfo known a Son
of a Knight of the Order, who had
alfo a Marfhal of *France* in his Family, fhew great weakneffes of
this

this kind, so that he was obliged to change his Condition, that he might not continue a Laughing-stock to others.

There are some who have more Honour than others, and who having once inconfiderately imbarqued themfelves, not being fit for it, do notwithftanding do their Duty, when they are once in the Army, as if they were naturally ftout; they fuffer very much, and I find that after having committed a fault, they can however be efteemed and thought braver than others. A Perfon of one of the richeft Families in *Paris*, having taken the Command of a Troop of Horfe, was in the greateft diforder imaginable when he was in the Army, he could not accuftom himfelf to the noife of the Cannon or Muskets, but took fuch diftafte at the Trade, that he took nothing that digefted with him; notwithftanding this,

C   in

in all things wherein he was commanded, he shewed no manner of weakness, but at his return from the Army he commanded his Valet *de Chambre* to fetch him his Cloak, and being the first who laughed at his own fear, told his Friends that he would be contented to run the Gantlet, if ever he was seen to wear a Sword again, unless upon a Journey into the Country, and so immediately resigned his Command to the King, and bought an Office belonging to the Gown, which he did not long keep.

This is what we must do, when we have made so little use of our reason, as not to think what we do, one Campaign is soon past over, and it is better to put some force upon ones self for a short time, than to be lost for ones whole Life; but the surest way is to consider of it throughly before we engage our selves. What I say here, is Calcu-
lated

lated for every body , and Perfons
of the greateft Quality may learn
by it as well as others : I know
very well they cannot live in any
great efteem without going into the
Army; but if I were in their places
I had rather chufe to live in the
Country upon my Eftate, than go
thither to be laughed at; for the
more a Man is raifed above others,
the lefs can he hope his faults fhould
be hid.

CHAP. V.

*Of the things neceffary for a Man
to know, before he goes into the
Army.*

WHen a Young Man goes firft
into the Army, there are
fome things that are abfolutely
neceffary for him to know , and
others which he may be ignorant

C 2 of

of without prejudice to his Honour; he ought to underſtand that
he is obliged to ſhew reſpeɛt to all
his Superiors, Civility and Deference to his equals, and to all Officers, and Love and Charity towards
thoſe he commands: But this kind-
neſs to thoſe under his Command,
ought not to reach ſo far as to re-
leaſe them from doing exaɛtly their
Duty, for in that caſe he cannot be
too ſevere. The knowledge of all
theſe Duties, will hinder him from
falling into great Errors: Firſt, he
can not ſhew want of reſpeɛt
towards his Superiors, without
being reprehended and even puniſh-
ed for it: The Generals always
taking care, that the reſpeɛt which
is due, be given to every one, not
according to his Birth, but to the
Command he is in: ſo that a young
Man muſt not, under pretence that
he is of great Quality, think he
may therefore fail of ſhewing all
repeɛt

refpect to a Soldier of Fortune, and
by yielding to him all manner of
Deference, he will do himfelf no
prejudice, and if he fhould fail in
it, would quickly be forc'd to it: Secondly, if he be civil to all his
Equals, it will caufe him to be
efteemed by all the World; Civility having in it the particular
Quality of gaining the Heart,
whereas Pride is loved by no body:
Thirdly, if he be refpectful towards
all the Officers, every one will fpeak
well of him, and he may hope as
well to make his Fortune thereby,
as by his great Actions; for reputation in War is often as advanta-
gious as any thing elfe: Fourthly,
if he has Charity for all thofe who
are Commanded by him, they will
undoubtedly love him, which will
be of no fmall advantage to him; for
when Soldiers love their Officer, they
will never leave him in any Action,
and will by their firmnefs make

him

him gain a great deal of Reputation. It is not the same with those who misuse their Soldiers; for besides that, they are very often shot by them in the Back, it is also certain, that the Soldiers being glad to make them receive an affront, will often give ground on purpose, and prefer their Revenge before their Honour.

We see therefore, that there is a necessity of being Instructed in these Four Duties, before we go into the Army, for unless we know them, we may commit great Errors; and it to be observed, that there is nothing more dangerous than to fail at the beginning: the first Impression which is given of a Person being always the strongest. I was made to take notice of the first of these Duties, the very first day I approach'd the Army, in a manner which surpriz'd me; I was a Cornet in a Royal foreign Regiment,

ment, and going to my Poſt, the Regiment being then in *Flanders*, I paſſed through *Arras*, where Monſieur *de Montaigle* who Commanded in the place, was ſick; I had Letters of Recommendation to him, and being deſirous to deliver them my ſelf, I went to wait upon him. He receiv'd me very civilly before he op'ned the Letters, but then finding I was an Officer in the Regiment, he took upon him a great deal of Gravity, and told me that Monſieur *Lombard* Major of the Regiment, was juſt come from the Army with a Convoy; That he had ſpoken to him of me, as of a Perſon who was recommended to him by a great many Perſons of Quality, and that I ſhould do well to have the honour of ſeeing him; Monſieur *Lambard* was Major of the foreign Royal Regiment, as I have before ſaid, and a very brave Man in his Perſon, but whoſe Merit was grea-

C 4   ter

ter than his Birth : so that I was
much surpriz'd at that word *Honour* , which I thought was not
used when a third Person was spoken of, but I was soon accustomed
to it; in a short time perceiving the
difference which was made between
a Captain and a Subaltern Officer.
It is not but that there are some
Officers who treat the Subalterns
very civilly , but since there are
others who make use of their whole
Authority; it is good to be prepa-
red before hand, to shew them the
respect that is due to them, by reason of their Commands. Monsieur
de la Cardonniere, when he was but
Commissary General, would never
permit any Subaltern Officer to
have his Hat on before him , nor
that the Captains of his Regiment
should sit down, unless he spake to
them. I have seen one of the Captains of ths Regiment, who was of
one of the best Families in *France,* and
of

of a haughty humer, be forced to do like the reft. Monfieur *Cardonniere* taking pleafure to ufe him thus, becaufe he knew him to be a proud Man. In the Foot the Colonels carry it yet much higher than any of the Horfe; for it is a Cuftom eftablifh'd amongft them, that none but the Captains are to fit down before them, the Subalterns always ftanding in their prefence, and moft commonly uncovered.

There are fome more effential things which a Young-man ought to know, when he goes into the Army; as never to turn his back, let the lofs and danger he runs be never fo great, for if he be once fufpected for Cowardize, he is irrecoverably loft. He had better fuffer himfelf to be taken Prifoner, which is the courfe all experienced People take in a general rout, there being lefs difhonour in it, than to run away with the reft. *Bonnet*, one of

the

of the Eldeſt Captains of Light-
horſe in the Army, and who
ſucceeded *Lombard* in his Command, after he was kill'd before
Eſpinal, told me this with Tears in
his Eyes ſome Months after the
Battel of *Taverne*; for they made
him reſponſible for his Regiments.
not doing their Duty there; and
in truth there was orders given before the Fight, to have a more particular Eye upon his Troop than
any others, and to disband it in
caſe they fail'd in the leaſt point.
The Commiſſary who was his friend
told him of it, and he being mine
made no difficulty of ſpeaking to
me of it; ſaying, that all his misfortune was, that when he ſaw himſelf abandon'd by his Men, he did
not ſuffer himſelf to be taken Priſo-
ner. Of all the Officers whoſe
Courage hath been queſtion'd, I
know but one alone, who has
advantagiouſly recovered his Reputation.

putation. He was Collonel of a Regiment of Foot at the Siege of *Lisle*, and I believe had not yet seen any great Action, so that not being accustomed to Fire, he shewed some weakness in the Trenches. His Father who was a Man of Courage, having heard what had happened, at his return loaded him with Reproaches, and the Son not daring to appear any more before him, took a Palisade the Winter following at the Siege of *Dole*, and would not quit it, till the Army had made it self a passage to go to the storm. This Action was so publick, being done at the Head of all the Commanded Men, that it made the whole Army speak of it, of which the best part applauded his Resolution, and the rest imputed it to his Despair; but in the Wars which have hapned since, this Officer having made appear upon all occasions, as much Resolution

lution as any in the Army; his invidious Enemies have been forc'd to yield, and he now deservedly passes for a Man as brave as any in the Kingdom.

The things which we may be ignorant of, when we go into the War, without dishonour, are those which are only to be learnt by a long experience ; nay sometimes there is an advantage in confessing one knows nothing : for those to whom we make this acknowledgment, will take pleasure to instruct us, to which they think themselves obliged for two reasons: First, to reward us for our Modesty: Secondly, to shew that they know their Trade. I have known an Officer of Horse, who after Twenty years Service, being commanded to blow up a Church, wherein it was said the Enemy intended to Fortifie themselves, ingenuously confessed that this Command puz-
led

led him, for that he never having serv'd in the Foot, he knew not how to charge a Mine. For this reason I am of opinion, that a Man who aspires to any great Fortune, must not be ignorant of those things; for if he hopes to be a General Officer, he must instruct himself in the Duty of the Foot, as well as the Horse, and go with them into the Trenches.

There are other occasions wherein it is not dishonourable to ask advice, whensoever one goes into the War: For Example, when the Enemies are to be charged, an Officer may take advice of those with him, giving his own opinion first, to shew that what he does is not out of Ignorance. This produces two good effects: First, it discovers often to him ways of beating the Enemy, which he did not think of: And Secondly, it encourages all those who are with him,

him, seeing he despises none of
them.

There are some general Rules
which every one ought to know.
It would look very ill for a Captain
of Horse in a Garison, to dispute
the Command with a Captain of
Foot; as a Captain of Foot would
wrong himself very much to pretend to command a Captain of
Horse when they are in the Field.
This is a thing establisht by the
Kings standing Orders, and which
is practised amongst all the Forces
of the Kingdom: yet I have known
the Marshal *de Schomberg* judge o-
therwise upon a dispute, which
happened between the Baron *d'
Ercé* in the Regiment of Horse of
the Chevalier *Duc*, the Chevalier
de Montecu a Captain in the Regiment of Dragoons of *Teßé*, and a
Captain of Foot. There was a detachment made of all Three from
the Army, to put themselves into

a

a Castle call'd *le Masdeou*, which is half way between *Perpignan* and *Bellegarde*. The design of Monsieur *Schomberg* was to hinder thereby the Enemy from being Master of it, and to secure the Convoys which came to his Army, which was encamped half a League on this side of *Bellegarde*. Immediately each of these Captains pretended to the chief Command in the Castle, and all Three brought pretty good reasons for it. *D'Ercé* he said, that the Garison being to march out as often as there should come a Convoy from *Perpignan*, the Command belonged to him; for they were to consider that the Marshal *de Schomberg* had sent them thither, only to be a security to the Convoys, and that therefore it could not properly be called a Garison'd place. *Montecu*'s answer to this was, that the Castle was inclosed with Walls, and that they being all Three there

till

till further Orders, they were to
do there as was ufed to be done,
when there happens to be Horfe
and Foot together in the Town: that
he being a Captain of Dragoons,
and the Dragoons rowling with the
Foot and Horfe: he faid there
could be no doubt made but that
he was to Command, becaufe he
was an elder Captain than the Captain of Foot; and that the Captain
of Horfe had no right to Command
where either of them was in a place
inclos'd with walls. What the Captain of Foot faid to exclude the
other Two, was that *Montecu's*
reafons held good as to the Captain
of Horfe, but not as to him; for
that his being an elder Captain than
him, did not conclude any thing
for him, for that he muft very well
know, that it is the Rank of the
Regiment which gives the Command, and that that of *Teffe* being
after his, it was his right to Command

mand without any Contradiction to be made. They could not agree it amongst themselves, and therefore desiring it might be regulated, the Marshal *de Schomberg* gave judgment in favour of the Captain of Horse. The Marshal of *Schomberg* might, if he had pleased, have prevented this dispute, by giving a Commission of Commandant to the Captain of Horse, before he sent them into the Castle, for then the two others would have had nothing to say. Howsoever this hapned, the wrong which was done, was to the Captain of Foot; for it is a general Rule, that the Date of the Commission signifies nothing in the Foot. For a Captain in the Regiment of *Picardy*, let his Commission be of never so late a Date, commands all other Captains, except those of the Regiment of Guards.

This

This was the only time that ever I knew this Order difpenfed with; but the Marfhal confidered that the Garrifon of *Mafdeou*, was only for the Convoys; which made him give his opinion as he did. This is a general Rule which a young Man ought to know when he goes into the Army, for he would be laughed at, if being an elder Captain in an younger Regiment, he fhould expect a younger Captain in an elder Regiment fhould be commanded by him.

It is not fo with the Horfe; for when there is a detachment made, the eldeft Captain commands, if there be no Major, for a Major commands any Captain. As to Subalterns, it is the fame in the Horfe, as in the Foot; for their Rank is according to the Antiquity of the Regiment, and not according to the Dates of their Commiffions: But all this may be learnt

learnt out of the Regulations the King has eſtabliſht, ſo that it will be ſuperfluous to enlarge upon this Subject.

I ſaid before, that it was the Duty of a Subaltern Officer to ſhew reſpect to a Captain. This ought to be underſtood alſo of all Officers in general, towards thoſe who are their Superiours in Commands; for we muſt not take the word in its plain Signification only, for then this Article would only concern Lieutenants, Sub-Lieutenants, Cornets, and Enſigns; and all Captains ought to ſhew great reſpect to their Majors and Lieutenant Colonels, and theſe to their Colonels, &c. When I ſpeak here of Majors, I ſpeak of thoſe of Horſe; for with us in *France* in the Foot, a Major doth not command a Captain, unleſs the Date of his Commiſſion be more ancient. To prove that this deference is due from us, to thoſe who

who are superiour in Commands
to us, I shall only recite here the
Kings Orders in that behalf, by
which the Captains are obliged
every Night to give an account of
the state of their Troops and Companies, to their Majors or Lieutenant Colonels; these to their
Colonels; the Colonels to the
Brigadiers, and the Brigadiers to
the General of the Horse, and to
the Commandant of Foot: which
shews plainly enough the Subordi-
nation, and consequently the respect which every Officer ought to
pay to the Person that commands
him. A Gentleman therefore must
not imagin that so soon as he is a
Captain, he may carry it as high
as he pleases. I have seen several,
whose Commanders have taken
pleasure to mortifie them, they having fail'd in this point, and I shall
relate here an Example which will
shew how dangerous it is for us to
fail in our Duty.   The

The Baron *de Vannes*, a Gentleman of *Lorain*, and a Man of great Merit and long Service, commanded the Regiment of *Gassion* in 1674. This Regiment being drawn up, *Vannes* gave order to a young Captain to advise the General Officer of something; but he thinking it below the Dignity of a Captain to carry a message, answered him, he might send a Subaltern, if he pleased, it being an employment much fitter for him: the Baron of *Vannes* told him, that it was him he commanded to do it, and not a Subaltern, and that he advised him to go, or else he knew how to make himself be obeyed; the Captain answered again somthing surlily, which put *Vannes* into a passion, and which came to be so great in them both, that they drew their Pistols, and were just going to give fire upon each other, had not the Officers of the Regiment
parted

parted them. *Vannes* feeing this, complained to the General, who immediately commanded the Captain to be fecured; after which, there was a Council of War call'd, which was juft going to degrade him of his Arms with difgrace, had not a Perfon of great Authority written to the General on his behalf, which ftopt the Courfe of its Juftice; notwithftanding it being a matter of Example, the Captain was forced to defire *Vannes* to intercede for him, which the Council of War expected he fhould do, before he had his Liberty, he being required alfo by the Council of War to ask his pardon, for what had paffed, at the head of the Regiment, which was to be drawn up, and at their Arms.

As there are Captains who are fometimes guilty of Paffion, fo there are Colonels who are as little Mafters of theirs; fo that

they

they often infult over the Captains
without reafon; but I have always
obferved, that although the whole
Army knew them to be in the
wrong, all the fatisfaction they
were ordered to make, was a few
excufes to the Perfons they had
offended. A Colonel, a very brave
man, but of a very violent Temper, and who befides hated his
Major, and of whom he had endeavoured by all the ways he
could to be eas'd, told him one
day, being both on Horfe-back,
that he fhould turn away a Wench
that he kept, becaufe of the ill
Example it was to the whole Army;
he had reafon at the bottom, there
being nothing in my opinion fo
unworthy of a Man of Honour,
as to carry along with him fuch
publick Marks of his Vice; but it
was not fo much the Scandal which
made the Colonel fpeak, as the
defire he had to be rid of him; for

a d·

adding many high words to what
he then said, he drew his Piftol,
and had certainly fhot him into the
brain, had it not miffed to give
fire; the Major made his Complaint, but all the fatisfaction he
receiv'd, was that the Colonel was
commanded to abftain for the future from fuch violent Actions.

We may infer from thefe two
Examples, what difference there
is made between a Colonel and a
Major, and a Major and a Captain;
we ought therefore not to fall into
this fort of errour, but yield an
implicit obedience, when we are to
obey, and command nothing, when
it is our right to command, but according to order, and for the
Kings fervice; for excepting in that,
the Subalterns may refufe doing
what is commanded him; for it
is not a Man's having a great Command, which gives them Authority
over them; for if they were obliged

ged to obey them in every thing, as well as in what concerns the Kings service, no Gentleman would serve in the Army.

Not but that I should advise all those who have a design to advance themselves, not to be too scrupulous; the services which we do for a Man of Merit in the Army, are not lookt upon as a servile officiousness; for if they were, the Generals would not have so many People crowd every day to make their court to them. It is sufficient not to shew the same respect indifferently to every body, without distinction; for it would not look well for a Gentleman, to do that to a private Captain of what Quality soever he be, as he would do to a General Officer; for that would look like a meanness of Spirit in him, for the deference he is to pay, is not to Quality, but to Merit; besides, a Captain

D   can

can do nothing toward the making of the Fortune of a Gentleman; whereas a General Officer can effect it, if he will undertake to serve him.

There are many young Gentlemen who go into the Army without having ever seen any thing, and who bring with them out of the Country, a mind puft up with Pride; for having heard it said, that there is nothing above a Gentleman, but a Prince: they think they should do themselves great prejudice to imploy themselves about any thing, but fighting the Enemy. These ought to consider the last remark I made, or at least, if they cannot quite rid themselves of this foolish Vanity, let them take care not to confound their Punctilio's with the Kings service. There are a Thousand Commands in War, which seem to be mean and servile, but which a Man cannot

not refuse to obey without making himself Criminal: you muſt fetch Ammunition-Bread if you are commanded, and ſeek out for Oats, and meaſure them, and diſtribute the Wine, and a thouſand ſuch things; in which we might commit miſtakes, were we not firſt informed of our Duty, all this being for the Kings ſervice. I have known Princes make up Faſcines, and dig in the Trenches, and yet it is not the imployment of a Prince to dig, or to make up Faggots.

Chap. VI.

Of the Duty of Subaltern Officers to their Captain, and of a Captains behaviour towards them.

I Have ſaid ſomthing in the former Chapter, concerning the Obedience, and Reſpect, which Inferior

ferior Officers owe to their Captains; but as there are other Duties which belong particularly to
them, it is not amiss to speak of
them here.   An inferior Officer
ought to have as much care of his
Captains Company, or Troop, as
if it was his own.   In the Foot
there is much less trouble than in
the Horse; the care of the Horses
being more troublesom than we
are apt to think; and in effect,
there may happen amongst them
every hour so many accidents, that
too great an exactness cannot be
used : Troops of Horse being most
commonly lost, only for want of
care, it is therefore necessary that
the Duty may be well done, that
each Corporal of a Troop, do every
day see the Horses of his Squadron, that he afterwards inform
the Quarter-Master what he hath
observed, he the Lieutenant, and
the Lieutenant the Captain.   The
Quarter-

Quarter-Master ought not to make his report, till he himself has seen the Horses, nor the Lieutenant; for when a Man has seen things himself, he can speak much more confidently of them, than when he speaks after others. When a Troop has marched, the Officers ought not to go into bed, till they have seen all the Horses, especially if they are to march the next Morning, because some of them may be so galled, that if care be not taken, they may be totally disabled. By this means the Horses will have time to recover, and the Troop be always kept in a good Condition. The Subalterns are so far obliged to this Duty, that the Captains may suspend them, if they are found faulty in their Quarters; they ought to go to the place where the Horses are water'd, that they may see them go backward and forward, for they may there much

D 3   better

better perceive whether they are
Lame or not, than in the Stable.
None but the Troopers themselves
ought to be allowed to Ride their
Horfes to water, although they
should have Servants, for none of
them are too good to take care of
their Horfes.   I have feen fome
who would give their Horfes to
their Landlords, and fometimes to
their Daughters to lead them to
Water; but a good Officer will
not allow of this, but take fuch
good order that they may never
commit the fame fault twice. They
ought to have a fet time to water
their Horfes, and the Officers ought
to be there fo as to fee them pafs
one by one, and if the Horfes are
all quartered in the fame Stable,
as it often happens in their Winter-
Quarters, they should have a time
fet for them to be dreft, and to eat
their Provender; that the Officers
being prefent, may fee the Gentlemen

men of the Troop do their Duties;
for the Proverb says, the Eye of the
Master makes the Horse fat. If
the Horses are separated, the Officers ought also to separate themselves to view them, and order
that their Provender be not given
them all together, but so as they
may see them eat it: for there are
some Horsemen, who are so disho-
nest, as to sell it, rather than give it
their Horses; but if it can be proved
upon any, it is Death. Any one of
these small Duties, if neglected by
a Subaltern, after the Captain has
commanded him, is a just ground
for him to suspend him. An inferior Officer being in the Camp,
ought also to take care that the Riders do not lavish away their Forage, nor be too sparing of it, out
of Laziness; for by too much sparing of it, their Horses fall in their
flesh for want of Meat, and by
being too lavish of it, they spoil

D 4　　　their

their Horfes, by going too often for Forage. I have feen fome Captains, and inferior Officers, who would rife in the Night to take care of this; and it cannot be ima-gin'd what a Reputation they got by it, of being good Officers. This is in fhort, what is to be faid, as to the care which is to be taken of their Horfes: But there are other Duties which belong to the Perfons of the Riders, and which a Subal-tern is obliged to take care to make them perform. Firft, he muft make them take care of their Arms, fo that they may be always fixt ready, and in good order, wherefore he ought to view them at leaft once a week, making them to be brought to him for that purpofe. All good Officers do this, and the Captains do not wholly truft to their inferior Officers, but are well pleafed to fee themfelves that there be nothing wanting. This ought efpecially

especially to be done the next day
after a wet days March, for if they
did not then take this care, the
Arms would be eaten up so with
rust, that if there should be a necessity of using them against the
Enemy, there could none of them
be discharged. The Chevalier *de
Fourilles*, would often ask to see
the Arms of a Troop, and if he
found them in good Condition,
he concluded their Officers were
good: Boots may also be said to be
of the Arms of a Horseman, so
that there must be care taken, that
there be nothing wanting about
them, for it misbecomes a Horse-
man extreamly, to have his Boots
without a heel, or unsowed, or
want a Spurleather; all which happens but too often for want of a
little care. There cannot be too much
severity used towards those, whose
negligence is the cause of this trouble to their Officers: but whatso-

ever

ever exactness the Troopers pretend
to, one muft not rely wholly upon
their own words; for it is to be
feared fometimes, they will infen-
fibly forget their Duty. An inferior
Officer is particularly obliged to
take care that the Horfemen keep
themfelves always cleanly, and neat
in their Cloaths; but it is very hard
to perform this in the Army, becaufe the Forage dirties extreamly
their Cloaths, and their Linnen.

Befides thefe Duties, there are
fome which refpect real fervice,
wherein the inferiour Officer muft
have a great fhare of Honefty ; for
a Subaltern Officer ought to be fo,
when a Captain leaving to him the
care of his Troop, trufts alfo in
him for his own advantages, making him the Mafter of all; for
there are a Thoufand things wherein he may cheat him; but he then
expofes himfelf to the greateft of
affronts, for if he be difcovered,
                                    he

he is not only forc'd in order to
reftitution to fell all his Equipage,
but lofes his Reputation for ever :
So that he muft never think more
of appearing in the Army, but muft
go hide his Infamy in the Country,
where he will not want alfo often
to have it thrown in his difh. There
are feveral Duties which concern
prefent Service, and of thefe there
are feveral forts; but of all inferior
Officers, there is required in none
more diligence than the Quarter-
Mafter. Firft, his Duty is, never
to go to bed till he has brought the
Word to his Captain, and if the
Captain be not in his Tent, he
ought to find him out, or ftay for
him there till he has acquitted himfelf of this Duty. He ought to do
the fame to the Lieutenant and
Cornet: and above all, let him take
care not to have too great an in-
timacy with the Lieutenant, unlefs
the Lieutenant be very well with
his

his Captain. That the Captain may not suspect they Cabal together against him; and tho the Captain and Lieutenant be very good friends, yet I would advise the Quarter-Master to avoid giving any manner of suspicion to his Captain; for suspicion is easily taken, but difficultly removed: Wherefore I would advise him to manage his ground as well as he can possibly, in all encampings; for if he lets another Captain have a House which belongs to his, his own Captain will have reason to take umbrage at it, and think he endeavours to make his court to another at his loss. The Duty of a Quarter-Master, obliges him to view the Quarters which are assign'd to his Officers upon a March, so that they may not have reason to complain of not being well Lodged, though it be but for a Night; all that he is to do, is to desire the Major, or chief
Officer,

Officer, to take care that they be well Lodged, and to reprefent to him the inconveniences of the Houfes they have already feen; but when they are to remain in Quarters till further orders, he ought to infift upon it much more; and if there be Troops already there, he may demand the making the Billets over again, that fome may not be better quartered than others. A Quarter-Mafter, if he knows his bufinefs well, need not be told it by his Captain; fo that the Captain may expect to find all things ready at his arrival: but if the chief Officers have quartered the Troops by diftricts and have left one for them, the Quarter-Mafter has nothing to fay, unlefs there be fuch an inequality in them, that the injury which is done to him is apparent; wherefore he ought not to complain till he has feen them all, when he goes to take

up

up Quarters with other Quarter-Mafters, and that they are to be quartered by diftricts; he muft view them all, that they may be equally good, and when he has thus equal'd them with his Camrades, he ought not to fuffer them to encroach upon his Quarters, upon any pretence whatfoever. A Quarter-Mafter, is not an Officer like the Lieutenant and Cornet; that is, I mean he has no Commiffion from the King, he being made only by the Captain; but when he has been once receiv'd as fuch, at the head of the Troop; it is no more in the Captains power to put him out, he being only to be cafhier'd by the King. It is not the fame with the Corporals, a Captain makes them, and turns them out at his pleafure, which makes them the more diligent in their employments.

One

One cannot fpeak fo certainly of the Duty of a Cornet, as of that of a Quarter-Mafter; but in my opinion, it is with a Cornet, as with a Voluntier; he is to learn what he can every way. I do not fee any fixt employment he has, except that of carrying the Colours, and provided he knows, that he ought never to take them, unlefs he hath on each hand one of the Troop to guard them: in my opinion he knows all he is obliged to know, as to his particular Office; but he muft not neglect the care he ought to have of the Troop, as I have faid before. I would have him be fo referved with thofe of the Troop, that he may not caufe a contempt of him: For the Cornets being ufually, hot and giddy headed young Gentlemen, it cannot be imagin'd the little value the Troopers have of them, even to the want of all manner of refpect
towards

towards them; fo that how young
foever a Cornet be, he muft know
how to make himfelf be valued,
and oblige thofe under him, to pay
him the refpect they owe; but this
he ought to bring them to, not by
feverity, but difcretion.

As to the Lieutenant, of whom
I fhould have fpoken firft, to have
obferved order; he ought to be
fully as knowing as a Captain,
their Duties being almoft the fame;
and he is often fent out upon Parties to Command, and to Command a Guard as a Captain; and
then having no body to advife him,
he muft have experience, for if he
runs into any error on fuch occafions, it will be ill for him. I have
feen fome of them committed to
the Marfhal, for having behaved
themfelves in Fight like mere No-
vices: wherefore I would never
advife a young Man, at his firft
ftep to be a Lieutenant, becaufe
they

they will not have the same indul-
gence for him , being Lieutenant,
as if he were a Cornet; besides,
the care of the whole Troop lies
upon him, and the Quarter-Master;
so that if the Gentlemen of the
Troop come once to find out his
incapacity, which cannot be avoided, they will neither have esteem
nor respect for him: and if so, it
were far better for him never to
be an Officer, than to be despised
in such a manner ; and his bad
Reputation will be quickly spread
through the whole Army : for the
common discourse of Soldiers, is
of their Officers, whose praises they
raise up to the Heavens, if they
esteem them ; but if they despise
them, they are sure to sink them low
enough : and indeed if one would
be informed of the Conduct of any
Officer, it is but putting his own
Soldiers upon talking of him, who
will quickly tell all they know
of

of, good or bad in him, with all the franknefs imaginable.

A Lieutenant or a Cornet, of what quality foever he be, ought never to take place of his Captain. I know very well there are fome, efpecially the Cornets, who do honour to their Commands; but I have feen thofe who were Dukes and Peers follow his rule, and the Captains were forc'd to take them by the hand, if they would have them go before them. Except to Perfons of this Quality, the Captains feldom trouble themfelves with this Complement, but always take the door before them. However if I fhould happen to have one of thefe great Lords for my Cornet, I fhould hardly take fuch ftate upon me, efpecially if they are civil to me; for thefe Gentlemen being Cornets only during one Campaign, and then rais'd to greater Commands; it would be great in-

indiscretion to use them so, as they might have reason to complain.

When the inferior Officers behave themselves as I have said, to their Captains: the Captains are obliged to use them well, either by treating them civilly, or by sometimes giving them some small Gratification: (for Example:) I never heard an accompt brought to a Captain of a Winter-Quarters, but he has given some present to him that brought it; and the inferior Officer ought not to refuse it, for two Reasons: First, because it is not so much the Captains present, as a share he gives him of the Kings bounty. Secondly, because it is a mark that he is well pleased with him, and he ought to be very glad that he lets him know it.

That which commonly breeds differences, between the Captains and inferior Officers, are matters of Interest; wherefore that they

may

may live well together, the inferior
Officer on his part, muſt be juſt
and honeſt, when he has had the
management of any thing left to
him; and the Captain on his,
ought to let him ſhare with him,
in the profits which are due, and
not take all to himſelf; he muſt
give him then what belongs to him,
when he has got any thing for
Quarters; that is, pay him for the
places in Money; in ſhort, do him
the ſame Juſtice, as he would have
done to himſelf, if he were a Su-
al tern. If a Captain does otherwiſe, he muſt expect that the inferior Officers will endeavour to
recompence themſelves another
way, and if there happen an opportunity of Plundering, they will
receive it with open Arms; it appearing the more juſt to them, he
having firſt ſhewed them an Example of taking the goods of other
Men. From hence ariſe the diſtur-
bances

bances and difcontents, which always end in the difhonour of both;
for when things come to be cleared,
and that it is known what it was
that made the quarrel, it will be
equally fhameful for them both;
that a fmall advantage fhould be
capable of deftroying the friendfhip,
which ought to be between them.
But notwithftanding any mifunder-
ftanding between a Captain and a
Subaltern, the latter ought not to
neglect the care of his Troop; for
he would deferve to be feverely
reprehended, if he did not endeavour to keep the Troop in good
Condition, and not in fpight to his
Captain, prejudice the Kings fervice, which he ought to feparate
from his interefts of whom he
thinks he has reafon to complain;
and confidering this, he ought
to do every thing, as if they were
the beft friends in the World. If
he behaves himfelf thus, it can
hardly

hardly be believed what Reputation he will get by it; for the more it is known, he has reason to complain, the more will he be commended for doing his Duty so well notwithstanding.

Chap. VII.

Of the implicite Obedience we owe to our superiour Officers.

I Have said before, that those who have right to Command us are to be implicitely obeyed; but since I did not then say, even where we know they are in the wrong: I shall prove it in this Chapter, by an Example furnish'd me by a brave Man, who for this was forc'd to leav the service, not to say put out of it.

Monsieur *de Pillois*, at the Battel of *Entzeim*, was a Brigadier of Horse; and reputed to understand

his

his bufinefs, as well as any Officer
in the Army; he had not yet charged, but ftood firm, expecting fix
great Squadrons of the Enemies,
which he defigned to charge in the
Flank. When Monfieur *de Vau-*
brun came to tell him it was time
to charge; *Pillois,* who was of a
contrary opinion, replyed, he intended to fight the fix Squadrons,
when they had paffed the *Ditch*;
and that therefore he would not
march till they came near it; but
Monfieur *Vaubrun,* thinking he was
bound in honour to fee himfelf o-
beyed; commanded the Regiment
of *Pillois,* at the head of which,
this Brigadier was, to march; and
Pillois thinking it would make him
lofe a fair opportunity, commanded
his Regiment to halt; and having
more power with them than Monfieur *Vaubrun,* did not advance till
he faw the Enemy near the Ditch.
Experience made it appear to Monfieur

fieur *Vaubrun*, that *Pillois* was in
the right, he having overthrown
them one upon another; but Monfieur *Vaubrun* having complained of
it to Monfieur *Turen* after the Battel;
Pillois receiv'd a fevere reprimand,
and if that General had not lov'd not
to ruine People, he had written of
it immediately to Court: but Monfieur *de Vaubrun* had not fo much
goodnefs for him, for not being
contented with the fatisfaction
which was made to him by the
Generals order, he made him quit
the fervice in a fhort time after.

If when we think we are moft
in the right, we muft however yield
an implicite obedience, much more
are we obliged to obey, when we are
commanded nothing but what
is certainly for the Kings fervice.
But I do not forbid examining the
commands which are given us; for
if a Man has a defign to betray
his Prince, and commands us to
                              put

put our selves into the hands of the
Enemy; it would be well done not
to obey him : but it is neceſſary
to be well aſſured of what one
does; for without that, one is reſponſible for the diſobedience. Excepting in this one caſe only, I
would not adviſe any one to refuſe
to obey his Commander, although
I once ſaw a Lieutenant rewarded
for doing it : He had been detach'd
with a Captain, to make good ſome
Pioneers, who were at work in
mending the ways; as this Captain and Lieutenant were at the
head of their Troop, they diſcover'd
about a hundred Horſe of the Enemy, which came to charge them,
they not being by one half ſo ſtrong,
which terrified the Captain, and
made him immediately reſolve upon a Retreat, and command his
Men to do ſo; but the Lieutenant
not approving of his warineſs, told
him he had no mind to run away;

E   and

and when he saw he could not
perswade him, he commanded the
Troop to follow, and to march
toward the Enemy; the Men cheer-
fully obeyed, and Fortune having
seconded his Courage, he routed
the Enemy, and far from being
reproved for his disobedience, the
Troop was given to him, and the
Captain cashier'd with shame.

It is true, this is an Example
which justifies that we may sometimes dispence with obedience
where a refusal is grounded upon
the Cowardize of the Commander;
but I look upon this as a verry nice
point: for if a Man happens to
be beaten, it is to be feared the
Commander will pass for a Prudent, and he for a rash Man. Success often justifies things, for he
is often esteemed, after having gained an advantage, who would have
been despised if he had been beaten.
However, I do not say that an Officer

cer who knows the weaknefs of
his Commander fhould not imitate
the Lieutenant I have fpoken of:
but before hand, he muft confider
a great many things. Firft, the
number of the Enemies he has to
deal with, that he may not undertake a thing above his ftrength, for
though one may leave a great deal
to luck; yet one ought not to expofe ones felf like a mad Man to
an apparent defeat. Secondly, if
the poft which he is intrufted with
be of great importance, and that
the lofs of it will draw after it
any ill confequences, one ought to
hazard much more to keep it than
otherwife.

I think alfo, that an Officer happening to be in a befieged place,
where the Governour defires to
Surrender, may refufe to fign the
Capitulation, if he thinks it difhonourable; but this is different
from what I have before related,

and

and it is not then difobedience;
for the place belonging no more to
the King, by reafon of the Capitulation figned by the Governor;
it is lawful for every one to prove,
or difapprove of what the Governor has done, efpecially fince there
is a Punifhment inflicted upon
thofe who refufe to fign the Capitulation, they being made Prifoners of War by the Enemy; but
I had much rather venture my
Liberty, than be faid to have done
a difhonourable thing. The Marfhal *de Schomberg*, commended very much a Captain of Foot, whofe
Name I have forgotten; who refufed to fign the fhameful Capitulation for the furrender of
Bellguard, which was made in the
year 1674.

CHAP.

Chap. VIII.

*Of the Punishments inflicted upon those
who refuse to obey their Officers.*

After having told the necessity
there is of obeying ones Officers; it will not be amiss to speak
a word of the Punishment, which
is ordained for those that offend.
As to private Soldiers, either in
Horse or Foot; it is a capital Crime
which is sometimes punished with
Death, sometimes with degrading
them from ever bearing Arms, and
sometimes the loss of a Hand, as
the case requires. (For Example:)
any private Soldier, who draws his
Sword against his Officer, is to
have the Hand which offended cut
off, and is to be degraded at the
same time from bearing Arms, and
sent home thus maimed and mise-

E 3   rable:

rable: and this is the reason that we see so many with but one Hand, which moves pitty in those that know not the reason for which they lost it. They are also sometimes punished with Death for the same Crime, but that is when they have either kill'd or hurt their Officer; otherwise they have only one Hand cut off. They are always degraded from their Arms when they Mutiny, but if the sedition be great, and prove of dangerous consequence, they can expect no mercy; for the Council of War then always condemns them to Death. There must be seven to judge a Soldier, besides the Major of the Regiment, who acts there in the nature of an Attorny General; none below the degree of a Captain can have a Voice, but all above. The President of the Council of War signs the Sentence, and when 'tis signed, it is carried to the General

of

of the Horse, if he be of the Horse ;
or to the Commandant of Foot, if
he be a Foot-Soldier, to know if
they have any objections to make
to it. That is to say, when they
are in the Army, where there is a
General of Horse, and a Commandant of Foot. I never knew any
act of injustice done at a Council
of War but once, but then it concerned all the Officers of the Army; which made them sacrifice a
poor unfortunate fellow, but it did
not touch his Life. A Regiment
had very good Winter-Quarters,
and had got a great deal of Money
for spar'd Quarters, as well for those
of the private Soldiers, as of the
Officers. The first demanded a
share in the profit of them, from
the Officers with Submission; but
seeing they were laughed at by
them for it, they mutinyed; and
one of them undertook to complain on their behalfs to the Gene-

ral, that he might do them Juftice;
and as foon as they were come
to the Army, he went to the Ge-
rals Tent with that defign; where
his Colonel unfortunately for him,
met him, and cunningly perfwaded
him to go along with him, promi-
fing to give him content: but, no
fooner were they got a Hundred
yards from the Head-quarters, but
he had him fecured, and carried
to his Colours, where making his
complaint againft him to a Council of War, he was condemned as
a Seditious fellow, and a Tale-bea-
rer, to be degraded from his Arms,
and to be Imprifon'd for Eighteen
Months.

This was the only time as I have
faid, that I ever faw a Council of
War fail of doing upright Juftice;
but all the Officers of the Army
would have been fubject to have
made Reftitution, had there been
any Countenance given to the Complaints

plaints of this Trooper, which
was the reason they all solicited
against him; that his Punishment
might impose silence upon the rest,
upon all other occasions. I have
always seen Justice as well admini-
stred by a Council of War, as by
the best civil Judges. The Articles
of War are read to the accused
Person, and he is asked, if he was
not informed of them before he
committed the Crime, and then
they judge him. The rigour of
the Articles may in some cases be
moderated: as I once saw it done
towards a deserter from his Colours, because he made it appear
they had forced him to march,
which had they not done, he had
never come into the Army. I
have known the Councils of War
exercise great severity; and a-
mongst others, one of the Kings
Life-Guard, for having deserted,
was Condemned to be Caned to
Death.

Death. This was for Example sake
to all the Guards, that the fear of
infamy might keep them within
their Duty.   This Guard was not
taken, but his Effigies was sent to
all the Provost Marshals, with order to endeavour to take him, and
if they did, to Execute this Sentence upon him.   Heretofore Officers had power of Life and Death
over the Soldiers, for any cause
whatsoever; and it is but within
these Fifteen or Sixteen years, that
the civil Magistrate has taken Cognizance of Robberies, or any other
Crimes, which respect the Publick;
but at present by the Article which
gives this power to them, the
King has declared he did not intend to infringe the Privileges
granted by him to the foreign Forces under his pay; so that they
are yet judged by their own Officers for any crime whatsoever;
but this does not make the Crimi-
nals

nals come off at an eafier rate, for
the Council of War is as fevere as
the civil Magiftrate ; and efpecially
among the *Switzers* , of which I
fhall here give you an Example,
having been an Eye-witnefs of it
my felf. In 1673. as I remember,
there was a Regiment of *Switzers*
engarifon'd at *Aeth :* a Soldier of
this Regiment walking out of the
Town , and meeting with a Maid
in the Fields ravifht her, and came
back in the Evening, as uncon-
cerned as if he had not committed
fo horrid an Action. The young
Woman all in Tears ran home to
her Fathers houfe , to whom fhe
made a lamentable Relation of what
had hapned to her. The Father
afflicted to the greateft degree im-
maginable , immediately came to
Aeth ; and defiring a private Audi-
ence of Monfieur *Nancré,* who was
then Governor there, informed him
of the violence whicht'he Soldier had
ufed

ufed to his Daughter; and defired
Juftice might be done upon the
Soldier. Monfieur *Nancré* fent immediately for the Commandant of
the Regiment, and having told him,
he expected he fhould find out the
Soldier; he commanded him to
draw up the next Morning his Regiment in Batalia, upon pretence
of a review, and leading himfelf,
the Girl from rank to rank, till fhe
had found out the Criminal, whom
he feized, and deliver'd into the
hands of his Officers to do Juftice
upon him. A Council of War was
immediately call'd by them, and
having interrogated the Criminal,
who was quickly convicted, of what
he was accufed of; they fentenc'd
him to be Buried alive to the middle, his two Hands tied behind
him, and that the Woman to
revenge her felf, fhould ftab him
to Death with a Dagger. So foon as
the Sentence was given, the *Swit-*
zers

zers carried it to Monfieur *Nancré*,
to know if he were fatisfied with
their Juftice, which befides his
thinking to be extremely fevere,
the injured Woman would not execute the Sentence; fo that they
were forc'd to moderate the feverity of it, and to change the manner of Execution, condemning him
to be hang'd; a Punifhment looked
upon amongft them, as the moft
infamous of all others : at the executing the Criminal, the Gibbet
fell down, which made all the
People cry out for Pardon, thinking this accident did not fall out
for nothing. But the *Switzers* Officers whofe Regiment was then
drawn up, being not willing to
allow a Crime of this nature to go
unpunifht, commanded the Executioner to finifh his Work, who becaufe, it would have required too
much time to fet up a new Gibbet,
knockt a great Nail into the head
of

of the wooden Horfe, and there
fulfill'd the Sentence.

But not to make a longer di-
greffion: it is fit to inform you,
that Martial Law is as fevere a-
gainft Officers, who fail in their
refpect to their Commanders, as
againft the common Soldiers. But
if it be wonder'd at, that there
are fewer put to Death of one fort
than of the other; the reafon of it
is eafily to be given, for the Officers are not fo much given to Drink
as the Soldiers; and without that
they would not commit fo many
diforders. For it is a fign, that it
is only Debauchery which fpoils
them, fince in the Army we fcarce
hear of their follies, they not having every thing in great plenty
there; but fo foon as they are in their
Winter-Quarters, is very hard to
keep them in good order. It is
not without Example that Officers
have been put to Death for
dif-

difobedience. Thofe that mutinyed
in *Treves* againft the Marfhal of
Crequi, were for that Crime condemned to die. Sometimes they
are degraded from their Arms,
when they fail in their refpect to
their Superiors, or break the Articles of War. He of the Kings
Horfe-Guards, who fent a written
challenge to the Duke of *Duras*,
was fentenced to undergo this infamy, not for having defigned a
Duel, for that would have been
Death by the Law, but for having
dared to challenge his General; but
he has fince been reftored, and made
Lieutenant to *Montecu*, in *Teffes*
Regiment of Dragoons. Thefe
forts of Punifhments are feldom
Executed upon Officers, becaufe it
is to be prefumed they do not deferve them, but upon the leaft
complaint made againft them, the
King cafhiers them. The Captain
has power alfo to fufpend the inferior

rior Officers, as I have said before, if
they difobey him in the leaft thing.
And this is done without much
ado; for 'tis but commanding his
Men not to obey the Officer he has
fufpended, and this is of fuch a
force, that it is not in the Generals
power to take off the fufpenfion ;
and he that is fufpended muft feek
his remedy at Court, for none but
the King can reftore him to his
Command.   I have feen many Examples of this ; amongft others, in
the cafe of a Gentleman , whofe
Name was *Crevecœur* of the Houfe
of *Gouffier* ; for all the intereft which
could be made by his Relations and
Friends could not prevail, and he
was forc'd to come to Court, where
he receiv'd as little fatisfaction ;
for his Captain having acquainted
the King of his evil behavior; the
King commanded him to quit the
fervice; but this coft the Captain
his Life : for *Crevecœur* having fome
                                      fhort

ſhort time afterward met him upon *Pontneuf* at *Paris*, made him
draw his Sword, and after a paſs
or two, kill'd him upon the place.

I have ſpoken of the degrading
of Officers and Soldiers; but I
have not yet ſpoken of the formal-
lity of doing it. Firſt they muſt
be Judged at the Council of War;
after which, the Criminal is brought
to the head of the Regiment, who
are at their Arms; the Criminal
has his Hat upon his head, and his
Sword by his ſide; but ſo tied,
that if he would, he cannot draw
it; and the Sentence is then read
to him, and when they come
to mention his Condemnation,
they throw his Hat upon the
ground, and take off his Sword,
not over his head, but pull
the belt under his Feet; which
when done, they give him three
blows on the breech, and ſo the
Ceremony ends.

I

I shall finish this Chapter with an Example which I saw happen in the Kings Guards, and a proof Authentick enough of the deference we ought to pay to our Superiors. A Gentleman near *Gournai* in *Normandy*, having a charge of many Children, sent Two of them to serve in the Kings Guards, and recommended them to Monsieur *de Ligneri*, who was then exempt, and is now Lieutenant of the Guards *du Corps*. Monsieur *Ligneri*'s Father was a friend to this Gentleman, so that Monsieur *Ligneri* receiv'd them very kindly, and having presented them to the Captain of the Guards, they had the Belt given to them. Sometime after this *Ligneri*'s Father had some difference with their Father about their sports, and he having informed his Sons of it, they began to use *Ligneri* as if he was their equal; and being engarison'd near *Paris*, one of them

passed

passed by Monsieur *Ligneri* without putting off his Hat to him, which made him run to him, and throw his Hat upon the ground, advising him not to be so unmindful of his Duty any more. Altho he was proud in his nature, yet he durst say nothing then of it, there being many of his Camrades then in the street; but keeping a resentment of it in his mind, in a short time after he desired leave to quit the Service, that he might be in a condition to revenge himself; but his design being suspected, it was proposed to call him before a Council of War; and if *Ligneri* had not interceded for him, he had run the hazard of being made an Example to all the Kings Guards: but not growing the wiser for this, he set upon *Ligneri* towards the *Rue St. Honore*, being both on Horseback, and wounded him with a Pistol-shot. The King being informed

formed of the matter, sent immediately to the Lieutenant Criminal, to proceed against him with the utmost severity, and to have him taken, if it were possible: but he hearing how the King was incens'd against him, fled immediately into *England.* But this did not at all hinder the Lieutenant Criminal from proceeding against him, and sentencing him to be broken upon the Wheel alive, which was Executed upon him in Effigie. And his Brother being suspected to have had a hand in what he had done, was committed to Prison, where he died for Grief, with seeing his Family so much disgraced.

CHAP.

CHAP. IX.

*That an Officer muſt behave him-
ſelf reſpectfully in the Generals
Quarters, and not ſhew any paſſion
there.*

THe Example which I have
brought in ſpeaking of *Ligneri*, makes it plainly appear how
dangerous it is, to ſhew a want of
reſpect towards ſuperior Officers.
But I ſhall go further in ths Chapter, and ſhew that we are obliged
to behave our ſelves with reſpect
in their Quarters, although they
are abſent. When I firſt came
into the Army, I could not
bring my ſelf to think that ſuch
caution was to be uſed any where,
but in the houſes of the King and
the Princes of the Blood: But I
was ſoon undeceiv'd, for I ſaw ſo
many

many punished for having given
way with me to this error, that I
resolved to leave it. The first Example which taught me my Duty,
was that of a Captain in the Regiment of St. *Lieu*, who being at
play in his Colonels Quarters,
in the haste he was to take up the
Money he had won; he threw a
great Candlestick against the Look-
ing-glass, which broke it all to
pieces. Monsieur St. *Lieu* came in
upon this, and asked him where
he thought he was, and he answer-
ing surlily, that if he was so concerned for his Glass, he was very
willing to pay him for it, anger'd Monsieur St. *Lieu* so much,
that the Captain was forc'd to keep
Prison for a Fortnight.

St. *Symon*, a Colonel of Horse
of the same Family, a brave Man,
and of great Reputation in the
Army, being at Monsieur *de Montbron*'s in the Hall, with many other
Officers,

Officers, took a fancy that *Brusart* a Colonel of Dragoons, who was at the other end of the Hall spoke ill of him, which provoked him to use several threats to him. *Brusart,* who was not at all inferior to him either in Courage, or it may be in hastiness of Temper; immediately put himself into a posture to shew that he did not fear him, and had not there been other Officers that hinder'd them from proceeding further, they would have endeavour'd to kill each other there. The noise which that made, having made Monsieur *Montbron* come out of his Closet, each of them would have pleaded for himself; but refusing to hear either, he sent them both to Prison, telling them, that when he had punished them for the fault they had committed, in quarrelling in his House, he would examin which of them was wronged, that he might do him Justice.

Juſtice. An Officer therefore, muſt have the diſcretion to know where he is, and if he has the Ambition to hope to riſe to ſomething, he will not be troubled to ſhew that reſpect to others, which he will be ſure to expect to have paid to him when he is in their places. It is not but that there are ſome unfortunate Circumſtances, wherein a Gentleman muſt needs be very much perplexed what to do; that is, when it happens that another puts an affront upon him, or talks of him to his prejudice. *Buſca*, who is at preſent Lieutenant of the Guards *du Corps*, drew his Sword in the Kings houſe, and wounded his Officer; who had given him a box on the Ear. It is true, he was forc'd to take his ſanctuary in *England*, where he remained for ſome time, but being at laſt recalled from his Baniſhment, notwithſtanding the fault he had committed,

ted , he was preferr'd to very great Commands. This shews us that sometimes we may swerve from the Rules. But I should never advise any one to take Example by it, since if we should even receive an affront from any one, the King has sufficiently provided by his Edicts, for the reparation of our Honour. I know very well that it is very hard to bear an injury, and that our nature inclines us to resist violence with violence; but when we consider that it is the Kings pleasure, and that besides it does not in the least touch our Honour , I cannot see why there should be so great a difficulty made of obeying. A Lieutenant in the Foot-Guards, whose name ought to be known to all posterity; in this shew'd a great Example of Wisdom: he had been sent to engarison to *Lisle*, soon after the taking of that place, and as he marched through the Town at the

head of his Company he made a
halt, and wanting a Pen with Ink,
to give some orders to a Serjeant;
he went into a Bakers shop, of
whom he civilly asked one, but
this Brute beyond all imagination; answer'd him insolently, that
if he had one, he would not let him
have it; and the Lieutenant endeavouring to make him see his
error in talking thus to him, the
Baker gave him a box on the Ear;
which insolence was no sooner per-
ceiv'd by the Soldiers, but those
who had Halberts were going
to run him through, and the
Musketiers who were within shot,
were making ready to fire upon
him; but the Lieutenant consider-
ing, he was in a Town newly
surrender'd, and where the King had
commanded the Garison to be civil
to the Inhabitants, hinder'd the
Soldiers from doing any thing to
him; and commanding them at
the

the fame time to march; he ftaid
at the door of the fhop till the
whole Company was filed off, to
hinder thofe in the Rere from doing him any mifchief, which might
have hapned had he been in the
Front. The King was foon inform'd of this action, which he
approved fo well of, that he gave
him the firft Company in the
Guards that fell. We may therefore very well conclude, that 'tis
the fureft way for us to do what
we ought; and fince our Duty
obliges us to contain our felves,
ought we not to ufe all our endeavours, that none may have reafon to complain of us. But to come
back to my Subject: I fay then,
we ought above all things, to behave our felves difcretely in our
Generals houfes; for befides the
Example which I have already given, I could bring a great many
more if there were need. The

fame

same respect is required in the head Quarters, which is properly the General's house, which puts me in mind of a thing, which I saw happen in 1676. The Marquess of *Rivarolles*, having won five hundred Crowns from the Marquess of *Feuquieres*, and he not being willing to pay it, he went to his Tent, which was near that of the Duke of *Luxenburgh* General of the Army, where after having made a great noise, he was going to have led away his Horses. The Duke of *Luxenburgh* being informed of the disorder; Commanded the Marquess of *Rivarolles* to be brought before him; and after having ask'd him, whether he did not know these were the Head-quarters, and consequently the Kings: the Marquess answer'd, he knew it very well; but to teach you against another time, replied the Duke of *Luxenburgh*, that the Kings Quarters

ters in the Army, is a place as
sacred as the *Louvre*: I must send
you to Prison, and immediately
did so, and when he had thus
punished him for his fault, he examined the matter, and forc'd the
the Marquess *de Feuquires* to pay
him the Money.

Chap. X.

*Of the severity of Martial Law,
and the Punishments incurr'd by
those that transgress it.*

THere are many motives
which induce Men to fol-
low the profession of Arms; great
Men engage in it, only to gain
Honour; for being born in plenty,
they have nothing left them to
wish for, but Reputation: but as
for others, who have not so much
reason to thank Fortune, they seek

to advance themselves by it; the hope of which, if taken away, they would be better Husbands of their Lives. Whether the motive which induces some, be the more noble than that which induces others, to take upon them this profession, I cannot determin; but they are all of them notwithstanding worthy of praise, for they all walk in the path of Vertue; and both these sorts of Persons are very useful for the service of the State, they spending their Blood for the Honour of it. But there are others, who instead of seeking to make their Fortune by ways that are Honourable, use all manner of ways to enrich themselves, which makes them commit rapin every where; and after having sucked the Blood of the People in Garisons, they endeavour also to rob the King, when they are in the Army, filling their **Companies** with

Fag-

Faggots, upon the days of Muster;
by which means a General is de-
ceiv'd when he is to give battel, and
finds his Army much weaker than
he expected. In all times there
were very severe Laws against these
Faggots, and against the Captains
who suffer'd them in their Companies; but the intelligence which
always was between the Commissaries and the Captains, made
them useless. This abuse had taken so deep a Root, that it requir'd
the Kings whole Authority, and
Monsieur *Louvoy's* vigilance, to remove it. His Majesty, made new Or-
dinances against these Faggots ; and
that they might be restrain'd from
this, out of the fear of the Infamy
which attended it , he commanded
that they should be burnt in the
Cheek with the Flower-de luce ,
and the Captains, who commanded
them , should be cashier'd without
mercy. And these Orders are now

F 4   executed

ecuted with the utmost severity,
he must have lost all manner of
Judgment, who for the lucre of
the pay of two or three Soldiers,
will venter the loss of his Honour,
and his Fortune: For let one but
consider well, and it is not difficult to comprehend, that one cannot long use this Trade, without
being taken in the Fact. A Man
who has been guilty of committing an ill Action, and knows that
his crime is known to another,
never sleeps out of the fear of being accused by him: How then
can a Man live at rest, having as
many Witnesses against him as Soldiers in his Company? Does he
not know, that there is not one of
them but he may mistrust, and that
to have liberty to go home, and the
reward which the King gives to
the discoverers, there will be some
one or other found to accuse him,
when he thinks least of it? But if

a

a Captain had nothing of this kind
to fear, for which he has reason
enough; methinks the fear of paffing for a bad Officer, fhould oblige
him to keep his Company full,
and he muft not flatter himfelf fo,
as to think he can hide his cheat
long, although he fhould have
good luck in the Mufter. For
when an Army marches, what
hinders a General from perceiving
the thinnefs of a Company, there
being many occafions for making
a ftop, to fee it file off. Then
there are no Faggots to be fhewn
to him, and what excufe can he
then make, when he is taken notice of; really I cannot imagin how
an Officer can have fo little Honour, as to enrich himfelf by fuch
bafe ways. There are others which
are more Honourable, and a Man
of fenfe will never advife him to
take thofe whereby, there is more
lofs than gain: befides I have feen
fo

fo many accidents happen occafion'd by this, that there cannot be too much care taken to avoid it; if I would, I could bring a thoufand Examples to prove what I have faid, but I fhall contentmy felf with two ; which will be enough to fhew that no body can efcape the feverity of thefe Orders. After the Campaign of *Maftricht*, the Commiffary Regiment having been fent into Garifon at *Lifle :* the Quarter-Mafter of the Colonels Troop, thought to pleafe Monfieur *de la Cardonnier*, who was Colonel of the Regiment, in making his Troop appear as full as he could. So that at the firft Mufter, he took Three of his Servants and placed them in the Ranks. A Trooper of the fame Troop, who had waited a long time for fuch an opportunity, to obtain his difmiffion, immediately difcovers them to the Commiffary; and the Servants

vants not being able to deny it, were sent to Prison: The Commiffary immediately wrote of it to Court, and receiv'd an order from the King, to enquire if Monfieur *de la Cardonniere* had contributed towards what was done; and in cafe he had, to give an acount of it without delay. Monfieur *de la Cardonniere* was not then happily for him at *Lifle*, fo that it was not difficult for him to make it appear, it was done without his participation; but yet notwithftanding he durft not fpeak in his Quarter-Mafter's behalf, nor endeavour to get a Pardon for his Servants. But the firft was cafhier'd after a long Imprifonment, and the others were burnt in the Cheek, although Monfieur *de la Cardonniere* under hand, made all his friends beftir themfelves to fave them.

The

The Example following, happned also to an Officer of Quality, which has something in it so strange, that I doubt not but it will surprize every body. Monsieur *Lucinge* a Brigadier of Horse, and Colonel of the Royal Regiment of *Piemont* was in Garison at *Doway*, where a Trooper of his Regiment in a Muster, which was made of it at the Gates of the City; came out of his Rank to discover a Faggot, which was in *Grimaldi*'s Troop. The Commissary, who was a friend to Monsieur *Lucinge* and *Grimaldi*, being glad to oblige them both, pretended not to hear him, and thereby gave time to the Quarter-Master of the Troop, to withdraw the Faggot from the Ranks, and to put him in the rear of the Squadron which was allowable; for informing the Commissary that he was a Servant who did duty like the rest of the

Troop,

Troop, he might pass him if he pleased, if not, it was of no consequence. The discoverer still pursued the Commissary to make him turn about, and he thinking by this time *Grimaldi* had had time enough to withdraw his Servant from the Ranks; told the discoverer, who demanded from him his dismission, and the 100 Crowns for reward of his discovery, that if he would shew him the Person he accused, he would presently do him Justice; upon which the Trooper would have conducted the Commissary to the place were he had left the Faggot: but his confusion was extream, when he found they had withdrawn him from their Ranks, and put him where the Servants are placed, who are in hopes to be allowed to pass Muster. He would have said something for his Justification, but the Commissary being the first to load

him

him with Reproaches, put it in the
heads of the Captains of the Regiments, to use him after the cruel
manner they did afterwards, that
all others might take Example by
him. They therefore gave orders to
Grimaldi's Quarter-Master, and some
others of his Troop, in whom they
most confided to take him out of
the Ranks as soon as the Muster
was done, and put him into such a
condition as to make him remember that days Work as long as he
liv'd. Monsieur *Lucinge* gave his
helping hand to the inflicting of
this punishment, so that when the
Regiment began to file off; the
Quarter-Master to perform what
was given him in charge, made
him come out of the Ranks, and
having made him alight, cut off
one of his Ears, after having beaten him with a Cane most unmer-
cifully. This poor wretch fled to
Arras, were he had his wounds
dreft;

dreft; and having related his mif-
fortune to fome of the Horfemen
of the Garifon, fome of them ad-
vifed him to go and caft himfelf
at the Kings feet, and to bear his
Charges for the Journy, they made
up a Purfe of a Piftol and gave him.
Being come to St. *Germans,* he took
fo well his opportunity, that he
got to fpeak with the King; and
after having told him, that he had
been a long time in his fervice,
he related to him his misfortune;
but the King would make him no
promife, till he had firft informed
himfelf, whether the thing had
hapned as he informed, wherefore
he gave orders to Monfieur *de
Louvois,* to write immediately a-
bout it; and in the mean while to
provide a fubfiftence for the Trooper, that his poverty might not
force him to return too foon home.
Monfieur *de Louvois* having performed what the King had Commanded

ded him, and having heard from good hands, that he had neither augmented nor diminished the truth in the Relation he had made; made his Report to the King, who immediately gave orders that a Council of War should be call'd, which he commanded to shew no favour to Monsieur *Lucinge*, nor any body else, but to do this unhappy Man all the Justice which he could expect from Men of Honour. The Council of War being assembled, proceeded according to the Kings directions, and after having considered maturely of every thing, they agreed upon this Sentence, *viz.* That the Quarter-Master, who had cut off the Troopers Ear, should be sent to the Gallies; and the Captains of the Regiments to pay the injur'd Person 600 Livers, and besides this, to conduct him in safety, and at their charge

into

into *Piemont*, and to anſwer body
for body for his Perſon, till they
had brought him home into his
own houſe. The King approved of
this Sentence, and to ſhew all his
Army, what was the Duty of all
his Colonels, he ſent back Monſieur *Lucinge* into *Piemont*, and
his Regiment was given to another.

If I had not ſaid, I would content my ſelf with giving theſe two
Examples, to prove what I have
ſaid: I would inſtance two that
lately hapned; one at *Calice*, and
the other at *Dunkirk*; but ſince
my word is engaged, and that
beſides, theſe are enough to inform us. I ſhould only ſay by the
by, that if *Mendoſa*, who commanded a Batalion of the Regiment of *Normandy*, had thought
of what he did, he had not loſt
the reward which he might have
expected for 20 years Service; and
                              that

that *Hofman* the Commiffary would not have been condemned to the Pillory; had he not been convicted of betraying his Truft. S. *Lo* and *Ardican*, would have been yet at *Calice*; the one Town Major, and the other Aid Major; if for fomething which was not worth their while, they had not caufed themfelves to be cafhier'd. The Correfpondence which they had with fome of the Captains of the *Switzers*, by giving them when they were mufter'd, Certificates of the Detachments, which they had made of fome Soldiers of their Company which were falfe, and which they did only to fhare with the Captains in thofe unjuft gains, was the occafion of their difgrace.

I fhall fpeak alfo in this Chapter of the Orders which Generals make when they are in the Army, and the ftrictnefs with which they caufe them to be obferved. They

give

give notice when they are to be
publifhed : After which, each Aid
Major informs his Regiment of
them, that they may be obferved
by them.   There is no lefs danger
in breaking thefe Orders , than
thofe eftablifhed by the King. Nay,
it may be faid, that the Juftice
done upon the offenders againft
thefe is much more quick and fevere, for without calling a Council
of War to judge the Offender; in
this cafe he is immediately hang'd
up upon the place.   Thefe Orders
are made upon many different occafions : (For Example:) Not to
plunder in a Country, which pays
Contribution, not to rob thofe that
bring Provifion into the Camp, not
to fet Fire to any place, and fometimes not to pafs beyond the Out-
Guards : It being a Crime punifh'd
with Death, not to obferve thefe
Orders , when once a General has
made them.   I have feen exemplary

plary Punishments , inflicted in cases wherein one would think so much rigour ought not to be used. When Monsieur *Schomberg* commanded the Army in *Catalonia*, they were two days without having any Bread, which made them all sadly complain. The General fearing therefore , that this want would force them to some violence; published an Order , forbidding thereby, any to plunder in any place, upon pain of Death , which kept the greater part in good order: But yet notwithstanding, a Serjeant in the Colonels Troop of Dragoons, in the Regiment of *Tessé*, not being able to resist his hunger ; found a flock of Sheep in a convenient place, and thinking he should not be discover'd, took one of them ; but returning back to the Camp, he met by misfortune Monsieur *Schomberg*, who seeing a Sheep behind him, ordered immediately the

Ex-

Executioner to be fent for, and that he fhould be hang'd upon the firft Tree. Monfieur *Teffé*, who was an intimate friend of Monfieur *Schomberg*'s, being informed of what had hapned, run immediate-to Monfieur *Schomberg* to beg of him the Dragoons Life, reprefen-ting to him, that he had a parti-cular concern for him, without which, he would not ufe fo much importunity, for that he had even forc'd him to come into the Army; after having taken him out of the Arms of his Wife, and that his Mother would never Pardon him, if he did not ufe all his endeavours to refcue him from the danger he was in, and that he would give the owner of the Sheep 100 Piftols; and al-tho it would be fomewhat dearly bought, yet he fhould own a par-ticular Obligation to him, if he would take it. Monfieur *Schomberg* hearkned to what the Count *de*

Teffé

Teßé said, with a great deal of coolness, but answer'd him more coolly; that he was sorry he could not grant what he requested, he being resolved his Orders should be punctually observed, and without hearing him any more the Dragoon was hang'd upon the next Tree.

In the *Holland* Campaign, the Count *de Chamilli*, a Lieutenant General, and a Man extreamly exact; Commanded a Body near *Mastricht*, he having publish'd an order for the secutity of those who brought Provisions to the Camp; a private Soldier notwithstanding his order, stopt a Peasant who had Bread in a basket, and took out of it a Loaf, which might be worth about Two-pence, and came back to his Regiment; and meeting with his Comrade, who was as hungry as himself, he gave him one half of it, telling him how he had got it:

Whilst

Whilst they were difcourfing, the
Peafant came where the two Soldiers
were, and knowing the Thief, he
went up to him, and defired the
Officers he might be fecured, and
Juftice done to him. The Officers
who fear'd the confequence of this,
if it fhould come to Monfieur *Chamilli*'s Ear, offer'd the Peafant a
fhilling for his Bread, which was
fix times as much as it was worth;
but the Peafant rudely refus'd their
Offers, and went immediately to
Monfieur *Chamilli*'s Tent, and made
his complaint. The General took
the trouble to come himfelf to the
Regiment, and forc'd the Officers
who had hidden the Two Soldiers,
to put them into his hands; and
making them draw Lots, although
there feemed but one to be Guilty,
and the Lot falling upon the moft
innocent, he was immediately
hang'd. Monfieur *Chamilli*, not
hearkening to any thing that could
be

be said in his Justification. Once relating this affair to the Prince of *Conde*, (he after having disapproved of this Action as being full of cruelty,) he did me the honour to tell me, he once found himself under some difficulty upon such an occasion, The case was this : A Soldier who was found without the Out Guards, after an Order was published to the contrary, made some proof to him, that he was there whilst the Order was publishing, and therefore could not know of it. The Prince told me that not to put an innocent Man to Death, nor to give ill Example to the Soldiers ; who would be brought to think that if an Example were not made , they might break such General Orders with impunity ; he ordered the Soldier to be hang'd in the dusk of the Evening, with a Rope under his Arms, but not about his
Neck ;

Neck, and when it was quite dark, he was taken down, and ordered never to appear any more in the Army. It is thus in my opinion, that Juſtice and Diſcipline ought to be joyned; for to think that, becauſe we are not to give an account of our Actions to any body, we may do any thing, is to load our ſelves to no purpoſe with guilt and envy.

The Officers themſelves are not exempted from puniſhment, when they break the Orders made by their General. The Marſhal of *Rochfort*, having forbid the paſſing beyond the Out-ſentinel of the Camp, ſent the Provoſt Marſhal with his Men, to hover about the Camp, with Orders to take all they ſhould find beyond the Out-ſentinels; amongſt the Priſoners which he took, there hapned to be a Lieutenant of Foot; who having a Horſe that was ſick, went to put

G   him

him to Grafs in a Meadow ; but
Monfieur *Rochfort* not being fatisfied with his excufe, ordered the
Provoft to keep him ftill in Cufto-
dy, and a Council of War being
call'd, the Lieutenant was cafhier'd
and degraded from his Arms.

Sometime after this, there hapned a like accident to a Colonel
of Foot, whofe haughtinefs coft
him dear ; for thinking that Men in
fuch Command as hew as, were not
bound to follow fo exactly the
letter of the Law; he undertook
to force through a Captains Troop
who was upon the Guard, and
endeavoured to make him obferve
the Generals Orders; drawing his
Piftol at him: the Captain on his
fide put himfelf into a pofture of
defence, but the fortune of Arms
being againft him, he was kill'd
upon the place. This affair made
a great noife in the Army, and the
King not being willing a thing of
                                     this

this confequence fhould remain un-
punifhed, order'd a Council of War
to be call'd , which would have
Sentenced the Colonel to Death;
had not his Relations pleaded, that
the caufe of his committing this
Action, was to be attributed to
Drink, which made them have fome
compaffion for him; but yet notwithftanding he was cafhier'd, and
was alfo forc'd to pay 10000
Crowns to the Captains Widow.

So that the difference which I
have feen made between an Officer
and a common Soldier for tranf-
greffing a Generals Orders; is, that
the one is punifh'd with Death, and
the other is turned out of his Command. It is not but that I am perfwaded a General may act more
feverely if he pleafes; but he commonly does not make ufe of his
whole authority, left he be thought
too fevere. Monfieur *de Ville*, in
his Book of Military Juftice fpea-

king

king of the Guards, tell us of
a Light-Horseman of the Kings
Guards; who was beheaded for
having attaqued a Corporal, who
was upon **Duty.** It may also be
said, this was not only to break
the Generals Orders; but to vio-
late what is most sacred in an Army; for when a Guard is set, none
of those which compose it, can be
affronted without danger, and tho
we had the greatest reason in the
World to complain of any of them;
our resentment must be kept till
another time. A very strange accident hapned at *Perpignan.* A
Lieutenant-of Horse, of the Regiment of *Brett*, and Son to the Major of the same Regiment; having
had some quarrel with one of his
Country-men, who had Listed himself in the Militia of *Languedoc*;
it hapned that as he was going
to the Army, he unfortunately
saw his Enemy, who was upon the
Guard

Guard at the Gate of the City, and not being able to master his Passion, he drew his Sword upon him and pursu'd him into the Corps *deGarde* ; but he at last recalling his Courage , and surprising the other with his return, ran the Captain through , making him fall down dead upon the place ; which for the fear he had of being punished for it, made him endeavour to make his escape, but *Ribertiere* the Town Major coming upon the place , setled his mind, telling him that if he was to be blamed for any thing , it was for not fireing upon him at first when he attacqued him ; and in effect, so soon as Monsieur *Schomberg* was informed of the thing , he was so far from proceeding against him that had kill'd the other, that all the proceeding was against the dead Man, to be an Example to others.

Chap. XI.

What a Young Captain ought to observe in a March, either to the Army or into Garison, and to whom he ought to go for Orders, either in passing through Frontier Towns, or when he is come to his Garison.

A Person who has never been in the Wars, and who gets a Troop either by the recommendation of some great Man, or by reason of his Quality; ought, (that he may not fall into great Errors,) to know what I am going here to observe. First, if it be a new Troop, and raised amongst his own Tenants, he ought never to suffer when he marches to the Rendevouze, any Soldier to straggle from his Ranks, under any pretence

tence whatfoever; becaufe new rais'd Soldiers thinking every thing is lawful for them to do, fail not of plundering of all fides, which caufes a great deal of trouble; he muft therefore, when he marches in the head of his Troop, place Officers on the Right and Left, and to bring up the Rear of his Troop, to hinder them from ftragling from their Ranks; and in cafe, they have any preffing need to go from their Ranks, he that gives them leave to go, muft take care to fee them come into their places again, that they may not take fuch pretences to commit diforders. At the beginning of the *Dutch* War, a great many young Captains very much repented their not having ufed this Caution; for the People which were plundered by their Soldiers in their march, fent up to Court long informations againft them, and when they expected to receive

G 4 their

their pay, they found in the Treasurers hands, the Kings order to stop wherewith to satisfie the injur'd People; and more over it is in my opinion to make a very ill beginning, to give cause to any to write against them; for what opinion will the King have of them, when he hears the first exploit they have done, is making War against the Peasant. A Captain ought not to allow his Soldiers in their march to speak loud, much less sing, for that does not become Soldiers at all: I do not mean but upon some occasion they may be allowed to speak together, but it must be softly, so as to shew they are sensible of the respect they owe their Officers, and that they are always ready to attend their commands. A Captain being about five or six Miles distance from the place, where he is ordered to Quarter, ought to send his Quarter-
Master

Master or his eldest Serjeant before,
delivering him the Kings orders,
that he may find the Billets ready
made out when he comes thither;
but when he comes near the Frontier, he must send him away in
the Morning before him, by reason
of the number of Forces which may
happen to be there; and the Major
and chief Officers must have timely
notice given them, that in so great
a hurry, they may have time to
provide Quarters for all. When they
are come before the Town Hall,
the order is to draw up, and to
face towards it, for it would be
ridiculous to face from it; but
yet I have seen some young Officers fail in this, not having been
informed of it. The Officers of
the Town ought then immediately,
to come down and pass them in
review, and deliver out the Billets;
but there are some, who make the
Troops wait; thinking that the Inhabitants

habitants. will thereby be lefs op-
preft, if they Quarter the Soldiers
a little late. In this cafe it is good
to put them in mind of the Kings
Orders, whereby they are engaged
not to keep them upon the Stones,
for this is extreamly prejudicial,
efpecially to Horfe, which are fpoil'd
more by this, then by marching.
If you perceive they intend fo to
ufe you, and take no notice of
what you fay, having an ill defign
in what they do, I would advife
the Officer to enquire where the
chief Officers have a good Meadow
and unbridle there: I have always
done thus, whilft I have been in
the War; when I have found the
Officer of a Town rude to me, and
I was no fooner in their Meadow,
but they fent to me and delivered
me out Billets. When a Captain
has his Billets, he goes to his own
Quarters, and draws up his Men
upon a Line before his door, the
Quarter-

Quarter-Master or Serjeants distri-
buting out the Billets, keeping a
List of them, that if there happen
any disorder, it may be known
who is to be call'd to an account
for it. This Counter-rol ought to
be double, one of the duplicates
kept by the Quarter-Master or eldest Serjeant, and the other given
to the Captain. When the Quarters
are setled, they cannot be alter'd
without leave from the Captain.
I know very well they venter very
often to do it, but no Captain that
understands his business will suffer
it. If a Soldier commits any disorder in his Quarters, the Captain
ought to make an Example of him;
and if he have kill'd or wounded
any body, the Criminal ought to
be deliver'd into the hands of the
civil Magistrate, to have Justice
done upon him. A Captain ought
to behave himself as I have said,
upon his march, until he comes
into

into a Garifon'd Town, for there he muft fend for Orders, or he will be made to do it. I have feen a great Conteft upon this account, between fome great Officers; one party pretending that only the Garifon was obliged to it, the other that no body was exempted from it; but it was decided that an entire Company Quartering in a Garifon'd Town, could not be difpenfed from it, and that, if the Recruits were not obliged to the fame, it was becaufe there feldom marched any Quarter-Mafter or Serjeant with them; and if there did, they had bufinefs enough upon their hands to look after the Soldiers, to hinder them from running from their Colours. It was alfo added, that the Governour had power, if he pleafed, to make all Recruits come for Orders, which was agreed to, by every body: fo that to fhew one knows what one

is

is to do, I fhould advife every Officer to fend to him for Orders.

If in a Garifon there happens to
be a Lieutenant General, or a Marfhal *de Camp*; then an Officer is
not to go to the Governour for
Orders; for that would make him
be laught at, and thought not to
underftand his bufinefs. The General Officer commands, wherever
he happens to be. This is a thing
paft difpute, and which I have
feen practifed upon feveral occafions. Yet I once knew a Governour, who did not know this, or
elfe was vain enough to give the
word to the prejudice of Monfieur
de S. Lieu, a Marfhal *de Camp*; but he
was jeered enough for it, and which
was worft, he had a Commandant
fent in the heat of the War, to
command in his room; by which
it plainly appeared, he was not
thought to be a Man of great experience. There happen'd a thing
in

in 1674. which, I do not yet
underſtand ; Monſieur *de Schomberg* , ſent to *Perpignan* Monſieur
de Mornas a Brigadier of Foot , to
take care of the Convoys, which
were to come to the Army, with
a Commiſſion of Commandant :
Mornas by vertue of that Commiſſion , expected the Gariſon
ſhould come to him for Orders ;
and *Chatillon* , the Kings Lieutenant of the Town , and Lieutenant
General of the Province, thought
it belonged to him. The reaſon in
all appearence was on his ſide, for
being the Kings Lieutenant,none but
the King himſelf had any Power over
him , but Monſieur *de Schomberg*
having taken part with Monſieur
de Mornas, he prevailed , and all
that Monſieur *de Chatillon* had
left to do, was to have leave from
the Count to retire home, that he
might not have the diſſatisfaction
of being forced to obey a perſon
he

he had always had the command
over. I cannot imagin why Monfieur *de Schomberg* declared himfelf in this manner againft *Chaftillon,*
for he knew that the Kings Lieutenants of Provinces, within their
Governments, command not only
Brigadiers, but Marfhals *de Camp,*
and Lieutenant Generals themfelves. Not but that there is a
diftinction to be made; for when
an Army is drawn together in any
County, the Lieutenant General
of the Army always Commands,
otherwife the Kings Lieutenant of
the Province always does, altho
there were a Lieutenant General
at the Head of a detached Party
to winter in he Country. The following Example will juftifie what
I have afferted. When Monfieur
le Bret a Lieutenant General, commanded the Forces of *Catalonia,*
and marched to *Bourdeaux*; Monfieur *de Montecu* the Kings Lieutenant

tenant of the Province would command, which the other did not take in good part, thinking the Command belonged to none but himself: almoſt all the Officers took part with Monſieur *le Bret*; but the Court, whither Monſieur *de Montecu* had written, decided it quite otherwiſe, which made Monſieur *le Bret* retire, upon pretence of ſickneſs.

But this Rule is not ſo General, but it admits ſometimes of an Exception: For Example, Monſieur *de Vaubrun*, who commanded in *Alſatia*, as Lieutenant to the Duke of *Mazarine*, being once at *Briſack*, Monſieur *de* St. *Abre*, a Lieutenant General paſſed by the place; he expected they ſhould come to receive Orders from him, but Monſieur *de Vaubrun* not agreeing to it; they both complained to Monſieur *de Turenne*, who Commanded in chief the Kings
Army

Army in *Alfatia*. Monfieur *de
Turenne* heard them both with
great attention, and then having
asked Monfieur *de Vaubrun* what
he was, and what Monfieur *de* St.
Abre, was; and he being anfwer'd
by him, that Monfieur *de* St. *Abre*
was a Lieutenant General, and
himfelf a Marfhal *de Camp*, Well
then fay Monfieur *de Turenne*, fince
the Order is, that a Marfhal *de
Camp* muft obey a Lieutenant General, pray do you another time
obey Monfieur *de* St. *Abre*.

An Officer when he is to fend
Orders, ought to know to whom
he is to fend them: It does not
indeed belong to him to decide
the pretenfions of any; but if he
knows his profeffion, he will do
well to fhew he does fo; yet in
fuch a cafe as I have mentioned of
Monfieur *le Bret*, and Monfieur *de
Montecu*, I would not advife a
young Officer to prefer a Lieutenant

nant of a Province, before a Lieutenant General of the Army; of the laft he will every day have need, and it may be he will never fee the other again in his Life. It is enough that for his own fatisfaction, he knows the Lieutenant of a Province commands a Lieutenant General within his own Government; but to make his court to the prejudice of a Perfon in whofe power it is to prefer him, is very abfurd and againft common fenfe.

When there pafs through any Garifon, any perfons of great Quality, I have known Governours order the Word to be receiv'd from them; the Majors muft in this cafe do what is commanded them by the Governour; but it would be a great fault in them, to go of themfelves. It is not for them to infinuate themfelves by fhewing fuch refpe&ts to any one, for they

ought

ought to own no respect to any, but, as they are distinguished by their commands, and as their Employments require a deference to be paid to them.

A Governour or a Lieutenant of a Province, coming to a Garison Town which has a dependance upon his Government; commands, although the Governours should be Lieutenants Generals in the Army. The reason is because a Governour or a Lieutenant of the Kings represents the Kings Person throughout his whole Government, wherefore it is very unfit, where the King is present, or he who represents him, that any other should pretend to command. I have seen a thousand Examples of this, besides what I have mentioned: As for Example; in *Picardy* and *Artois*, the Duke of *Elboeuf* commands when he is at St. *Quintin*, and Monsieur *de Pradel* a Lieutenant General

ral and Governour of the place obeys him; as also *Nancré* and all others that are Lieutenant Generals; nay more if the Marshal *de Crequi*, Governour of *Bethune* were in his Government, though he be a Marshal of *France*, he must be commanded by the Duke of *Elbeuf*, for in this case, that Quality is not consider'd; there must notwithstanding be a distinction made, which is very remarkable, which is, that when an Army is drawn together in a Province; the Person who has the Kings Commission to command in chief, commands every where, which caused Mon-*de Turenne*, to give his opinion against *Vaubrun*, in the dispute between him and St. *Abre*; because the Kings Army being in *Alsatia*, he was to obey Monsieur *de* St. *Abre*, as well at *Brisack*, as in the Army. This remark has great need to be cleared, because of what

I

I have said before of Monsieur *de Montecu* , and Monsieur *le Bret* ; for there are many who will not be able to comprehend the reason without it , why Monsieur *de Vaubrnn* was to obey Monsieur St. *Abre*, and yet *Montecu* was to command *le Bret*. But you will find this difference in their cases. First, Mon. *de Vaubrun* was an Officer in the Army, and it would have been going against all Order, to have him command a Man who is naturally to command him , for the Employment he had in *Alsatia* , was not to be taken notice of in relation to Monsieur *de* St. *Abre*. If Monsieur *de Montecu* had been a Marshal *de Camp* in the Army of *Catalonia*, as Monsieur *de Vaubrun* was in that of *Alsatia* ; without dispute it would not have becom'd him to have disputed with Monsieur *le Bret* for the command; but he was barely the Kings Lieutenant in that

that Province, and he claimed the command in Right of his Office. Secondly, there is also this difference; that Monsieur *de St. Abre*, was in a Province where the Kings Army acted, and therefore he had all sorts of command there; and Monsieur *le Bret* on the contrary was in a Country that was quiet, and where the Troops were come to take their Winter-Quarters. Therefore there could be no manner of reason to think, that the Kings Lieutenant of a Province, who in the Governours absence represents the Kings Person, should receive Orders from him.

All the Kings Lieutenants of Provinces commanding, as, I have said even Lieutenant Generals of the Army within their own Governments. They are when they there view any Forces to be saluted with the Sword by the Horse, and with the Pike by the Foot, the Kings Guards excepted; for they

owe

owe no salute , but to the King himself,if they do otherwise towards the Generals , it is because they sometimes to make their Court dispence with their Duty. Whilst the Marshal *de Albret* commanded the King's Gendarms : I saw, Monsieur *de la Salle* , who was a Sub-Lieutenant under him,beat a Trumpeter for sounding a March at his coming to the head of the Squadron ; he also forbad the Gendarms to draw their Swords , and the Marshal durst not take notice of it, for he knew that respect did not belong to him ; Monsieur *de la Salle* and he, were then at odds, or else I believe Monsieur *de la Salle* would not have used so much formality. When one *Roure*, headed a Rebellion in *Vivarez* , Monsieur *le Bret* had Orders to march against him. The Count of *Roure*, the Kings Lieutenant of *Languedoc* , and who had *Vivarez* within

his

his Commiffion, fent him word he intended to come in Perfon to the head of the Forces. This troubled Monfieur *le Bret*, that he fhould be forc'd to obey a Man of but Two and Twenty years of Age; but, there being no way to avoid it, he went to him, for Orders, and made him be faluted when he took the command of his little Army. I have notwithftanding, known fome Old Officers do otherwife, and not falute a Lieutenant of a Province; but I would not take Example by them, for they have been always forc'd the next day to make excufes for it to him, and make ufe of fome pitiful reafons to extenuate their fault.

Men who are poffeft of any of thefe great Commands, take great care not to do any thing beneath them, nor to fuffer any omiffion of the refpect which they think is due to them, in others. So that

I

I would not advise any to make themselves a business of this nature, for they are not like to come out of it with much honour; besides, those Persons always remember any affronts done to them, and they being in great Authority, it is dangerous to incur their displeasure. Nay, they will not yield up their Rights in any dispute with the Clergy, and Monsieur *de Bar*, Governour of *Amiens*, had a long suit with the Bishop, who pretended all the Chapter was to be *Incens'd* in the Church before him; and Monsieur *de Bar*, claim'd it as his right to be *Incens'd* immediately after the Bishop; there were great Factions made to support each side, and the Bishop of *Amiens* forgot not to use his Rhetorick. But for all that, the matter was judged in Council, the King present, in favour of Monsieur *de Bar*, and all other Governours, do now follow this

H   order,

order, altho I have had it from
very good hands, that before this
feveral of them refufed to joyn
with him, in following the fuit.

CHAP. XII.

*Of what an Officer is to obferve,
being in the Enemies Country.*

I Will not pretend here to lay
down a General Rule for his behaviour, which is impoffible in any
Condition, efpecially that of a Soldiers, in which the Situation of the
place often determines the Refolution which is to be taken, and the
number of the Enemies muft in-
ftruct him what courfe to take;
but there are fome Rules to be
obferved, *viz.* The place or number of the Enemies: For Example,
an Officer at the head of a Troop
of Horfe in a March, would fhew

a

a great want of skill to skirt a
Wood, for he muft march as far
from it as he can, for the ftrength
of Horfe is in an open Country, as
that of the Foot is in the Woods.
It is not that I would have an Officer of Foot incommodate his
march, by marching fo near a
Wood; for Ambufcades of the
Enemy, are always to be feared
in fuch cafes. It is alfo then
dangerous for a Troop of Horfe,
becaufe they may fall upon him,
and cut him off before he can get
to a fecure Poft. An Officer of
Foot therefore marching through
an inclofed woody Country, muft
have the difcretion not to march
in the middle of the Plains, nor
too near the Woods; by this means
he will have time to chufe what
courfe to take, fo as to hinder himfelf from being beaten; or at leaft if
he be beaten, it will not be for want
of ufing the rightforms; if he be

H 2   at-

attacqued by Horse, he ought to Retreat into the Wood, and skirmish till he be got into it; for if he have time enough to throw himself into it; he may be assured he will not be attacqued, if he have to deal with Foot, and that he is the weakest, he must endeavour to regain the last defile, and putting himself in Batalia in the Rear, he must dispute every Foot of ground as much as he can; but if he sees he cannot hold long without being routed, he must retreat still to some other defile, Sacrificing five or six Soldiers to cover his retreat. The Horse being prest hard, ought to follow the same method, so that when one marches in an Enemy's Country, one must observe the places one passes through, as exactly as curious Travellers do, so as not to be mistaken in passing; so that it may very well be said, that when an Officer has any share of understanding, and knows the
Country,

Country, it is almost impossible
for him to be beaten, in marching:
an Officer ought to send out Scouts
before him, instructing them what
they are to do; the duty of Scouts
not being to advance full speed
towards the Enemy, as many do
with great imprudence. But if they
discover any thing, they are presently to give an account to the
Commander in chief, and waiting
for his Orders, not to march faster
than a foot pace; when they have
Orders to Charge, they must go
upon the Trot, for that awakens
the mind, and animates the Courage. When the Scouts pass through
a Village, it must not be without
making diligent enquiry and search,
for there may be a party of the
Enemy there; who to have
the more advantage, will let
them pass by, and not discover
themselves, till they can fall upon
their Body. That which the Of-

H 3   ficer

ficer who Commands them, ought
to do in this cafe, is, to take one
or two of the Village, and to enquire of them, if there be any
news; if they anfwer him, there
is not, as moft commonly they do,
he is not for all that to truft to
their Word, but carry them with
him beyond the Village, that they
may be hoftages for him; for this
is a way to make them fpeak the
truth, and he ought not to releafe
them, till he fees his own party
fafe; wherefore he is to ftay till
the whole Troop be within Muf-
ket fhot on the farther fide of the
Village, and if it happens that the
hoftages have deceived them, it is
lawful for him, by the Law of
Arms, to kill them upon the place:
a Man that is at the head of a
Troop, ought to detach but one
prudent Man to command his
Scouts; if thefe Scouts are but 12
or 15, they fend out only 2 before
them,

them, and these two ought to look on all sides of them; if any thing appears, they must go upon the Trot, to ask upon any discovery, who they are for. The Scouts make them good, and the Troop supports the Scouts, the strongest commonly make the weaker-give the Word; but there are some so obstinate, that they will not answer, which has been the cause that many times people of the same party have charged each other. *Du Brvil*, a very rich Man, who carried the White Colours, was unfortunately kill'd in 1667. upon the like occasion; so that to prevent any such accidents for the future, the King made an Order, that the weakest party should be obliged to speak first, which it may be is the least obeyed of any, every one looking upon it as a point of Honour, to make the other party to speak first. When one marches

H 4   thus

thus in an Enemies Country, it is more safe to Encamp, than to stop in any Village; for the Soldiers cannot find at the corner of a Hedge, as they do in a House wherewithal to Debauch; for if they can, they had rather be hang'd than not drink all Night; so that if any thing should happen to require their immediate service, they must not be kept wallowing in plenty, though it were in our power; for they are much readier for service when they suffer some little want, than when they enjoy too much plenty.

When an Officer is arriv'd where he is resolv'd to Encamp, he must draw up his Men, and having set his Guards, he may give his Men some ease, by allowing them to alight from their Horses, if it be Horse, or if Foot, to repose themselves; but they must always be fac'd towards the Town, which

is

is nearest the Enemy, leaving as much as may be a defile in the Front and Rear, which are to be guarded to prevent a surprize; if the danger be imminent, they must be kept at their Arms all Night; and for greater security, Scouts are to be sent out from Half-hour to Half-hour, and at day break Scouts are sent out further than those which went out in the Night; and when they are come back, the March is to be continued. I would advise the Foot to lye in the Woods, when they are to march 2 or 3 days in the Enemies Country, for thereby they run much less hazard; the Horse may also do the same, that they may not be so soon discovered; but it is necessary for both to traverse the Wood well before they engage themselves in it, for there may be Ambuscades laid, to which they may fall when they least think of it.

I

I have known Officers, who for not having taken these cautions, have been beaten by their own fault; wherefore a Captain ought not to suffer his Men to straggle, because he is near the place whither he is ordered to go; it is there where the Enemy most commonly lays his Ambuscades, thinking as it happens too often, that by too great a confidence, not to say negligence, they shall find Men in most disorder. In our return from the Campaign of *Lisle*, the forces which accompanied Monsieur *de Turene* to *Doulens*, quitted their Squadrons and Battalions, so that there happening an alarm, there could hardly enough be found to make out a regular detachment; the Officers having been the first to leave the head of the Troops: Monsieur *de Lamezan*, who had lately sold his Command of Sub-Lieutenant of the Gendarms to the

the Prince of *Soubife*, was also kill'd in the fame place, by the fault of the Commander of his Convoy; for he had no fooner difcovered the Steeples of the Town, but he fuffer'd his Men to ftraggle, thinking himfelf in fecurity; but foon after being fet upon, he was forc'd to run away, and thofe who ftood their ground were all kill'd upon the place. It is therefore a very dangerous thing to fuffer thofe one Commands to leave their Ranks; for were there no danger, does it look well for an Officer to come to the Gates of a Town with half his Troop, and to be forc'd to enter it without them, or to ftay till they are come up? When an Officer does this, he muft not expect to gain much Reputation, nor even to be the better beloved by his Soldiers; for although the liberty which he gives them, is pleafing to them, for the prefent

fent they are apt to defpife him;
afterwards he thereby fhewing that
he knows not how to acquit himfelf
of his duty as he ought.

An Officer muft take care not
to take any falfe alarm; that is,
think he fees the Enemy when
he fees only Cattel or Trees;
for although that may proceed
from a badnefs of fight, yet Men
who are always apteft to believe
the worft, will attribute it to fear;
which when they once believe,
'tis very hard to remove fuch im-
preffions; he muft therefore never
be pofitive in any thing, till he
be affured he cannot be deceived.
Yet I have known Officers, who
commanded the Scouts, fend word
that they had difcovered the Enemy; and when the chief Officers
of the body of the Army came
up to fatisfie themfelves, they
found, they appeared only in their
own imagination; when this has
once

once hapned to an Officer, he is laught at for it all his Life time, and he cannot think ever to be excufed it. A Man ought therefore never to report any thing which he has not feen himfelf, for he muft not truft to any body elfe in this cafe: It being but an ill excufe for a Man to make for giving a falfe alarm, to caft the fault upon another.

A Lieutenant in the Regiment of *Chau,* who was fubject to thefe fort of Vifions, was once fent out to make good the Scouts, and was followed by much a ftronger Troop than that which he commanded; the Country where he marched, was all divided with Ditches, and Hedges; fo that one could not march very far without meeting with a great many Lanes; and there fell fo great a ftorm of Rain, that a Ditch over which the Scouts had paffed, was fill'd with water,

fo

so that endeavouring to pass it, he
escaped drowning very narrowly;
he therefore drew up his Squadron,
and casting his Eyes on the other
side, he took a fancy that he saw
the Enemy charging the Scouts,
and putting them to the Rout;
the Rain being ceased, he perceived afar off, upon the side of
a high way, a little Shepherds Cot,
and a Sheep-fold; there stood also
there three Carts loaded with
Corn, which were brought to the
Barn; the Carts, he took for so
many Squadrons, and the Fold for
a Battalion, which made him send
word to him that was to strengthen
his party; that his Scouts were
either kill'd or made Prisoners, and
that it was best for him to Retreat
quickly, the Enemy being by much
the strongest: The Commander of
that party being a young Man
without experience, relyed wholly
upon his information, and returned
without

without making any further inquiry; being come back to the Camp, he made his Report of what had hapned, to the General; and posseſt every body ſo much with the imaginary danger he had been in, that every body lookt upon him as happily eſcaped; but by misfortune for him, whilſt they were ſpeaking of the Scouts which were thought to be kill'd, they came back to the Camp to the great ſurpriſal of all; every one running to them, to know how they had eſcaped from ſo great a danger, but being anſwer'd, that they had ſeen none, it was eaſily ſeen that all the fault was in the Officers; ſo that the thing being reported to the General, he commanded them both to be ſecured in the Cuſtody of the Provoſt Marſhal, being reſolved to proſecute them: but ſome friends interceding for the Priſoners, they were taken out of the
hands

hands of the Marshal; but it was upon condition they should appear before the Council of War, at which the Captain and the Lieutenant were cashier'd, and it was like to have gone worse with the last; for by assuring that the Scouts had been beaten, he had spoken ill of a Cornet who commanded them, who was a young Gentleman of Quality, and took the thing much to heart; and indeed a Man ought not only to take care of his Actions but his Words, for he must not with impunity take away any Man's Reputation by his obloquy.

As it is dangerous to take a false alarm, it is not a less one to engage ones self imprudently in danger, because imprudence tarnishes the bravest Actions, for both are equally blamed, as the following Example will shew. The Marquess of *Genlis*, Colonel of the Crown Regiment, being

being arrived at *Tongres*, in 1673.
obtained a Convoy to go as far as
Maseik; there were Fifty Horse
commanded out with a Captain,
Lieutenant, Cornet, and Quarter-
Master; when the Troop was out
of the Town, the Captain detach'd
his Scouts, commanded by a Cornet of the Commiffary Regiment,
a very brave Man; but whose
Head went faster than his Arm, fo
that without reflecting how he
engaged himself, he enter'd upon
a *Causey* without discovering on
both sides of it; by that time he
had got 200 yards, he perceived
upon his Left-hand a great Squadron, and before him 50 or 60
Men, who were lying upon their
Faces, and who arose up assoon as
they saw him engaged upon the
Causey; he immediately commanded his Men to halt, and thought
to have Retreated back; but he
found behind him a like number
of

of Foot, who prefented their Muskets at him : in this extremity he
took that courfe which his Courage infpir'd him with, which was
to charge thofe in the Front; and
Fortune feconding his boldnefs, he
routed them , and kill'd the Commander with his own Piftol , from
thence he went on to *Mafeick*, whilft
the Marquefs of *Genlis* , who was
an Eye-witnefs of this Action,
thinking it not proper to engage
fo many of the Enemy, returned
back to *Tongres*, where he gave fuch
a Relation of what had hapned , as
gave caufe enough to commend
the Courage and blame the imprudence of the Cornet.

In fpeaking above , I faid the
Lieutenant was very like to
have been punifhed feverely, for
having accufed a Cornet for not
doing his duty ; an Officer muft
therefore take great care to abftain from fpeaking ill of any body,
for

for flander is fo odious to all People, that altho we naturally love
to hear ill of our Neighbour, yet
he is always fure to be efteemed
by none that fpeaks it; and befides, it will be impoffible for him,
not to caufe himfelf thereby a
thoufand quarrels; for thofe who
thus tear their Neighbours Reputation, have always a defign in it;
they thinking by pulling down the
honour of others, they fhall raife
themfelves upon their Enemies;
but they do not take notice that
it will happen the quite contrary
of what they think; for inftead of
gaining thereby efteem, they create
in all an evil opinion of their virtue,
Men commonly not contenting
themfelves with words, to give
their efteem, for great Actions
alone can acquire it; and I have
always obferved, that they that
never fpeak ill of their Neighbours
are commonly the honefteft Men.

Mon-

Monſieur *de Turene* could never endure to hear any one ſpeak ill of another; and I have often heard him take the parts of Men very little known to him, and reprove thoſe who ſpake ill of them, and to prevent the accuſing an Officer of Cowardize, who had the misfortune of being once beaten; he would give him the Command of another party, and if he then hapned to come off again with loſs, he would ſtill ſend him out till he had his revenge; and then taking pleaſure to juſtifie him, would ſpeak of his laſt Actions in ſuch terms, as were able to deſtroy any ill opinion that was formerly conceived of him : he alſo always maintained, that a Man ought not to be the leſs eſteemed of, for having been beaten; for if that were a good rule, he ſaid he was ſure his Reputation was loſt long ago.

CHAP.

CHAP. XIII.

What a young Officer is to do when he comes into the Army.

WHen a Man has never been in an Army, when he comes into the Camp, he is in an amazement, he hears a Language fpoken, which till then, was unknown to him; and to which before he is accuftomed, he muft be fome time in the Camp. The Guard of the Camp, the *Piquet*: The Guard of the Colours: The Orderly Guard: The Generals Guard: The Main Guard: The Ordinary Guard: And the *Bivac*, are new Words to him; and which he cannot underftand the meaning of, until they are explained to him. The Guard of the Camp, is the Guard upon which the whole Army

Army relies; they have Day-posts,
and Night-posts; their Posts in the
Day time are at some distance from
the Camp, and on the side which
is towards the Enemy, that if any
thing appears, the Army may have
timely notice to stand to their
Arms; their Posts at night are
near the Army, that they may
not be cut off by the Enemy ; in
the day time this Guard commonly alight from their Horses, and
detach a small Corps-de-guard before them, and that small Guard
Centries sometimes one sometimes
two as need requires. This small
Corps-de-guard do also alight from
their Horses, the Sentinels only
being on Horseback, which are relieved every hour; there is also
a Sentinel plac'd on the side towards
the Army, but this is only to give
notice when the Generals are coming, for then the whole Guard is
obliged to be on Horseback, and
to

to receive them with their Swords drawn, unless there be an express Order to the contrary; the Persons to be saluted with the Sword, are the Generals, the Lieutenant Generals, the Marshalls *de Camp*, and the Generals of Horse; for when any of these appear, this respect is to be paid to them : in the Night-time the Guard ought never to a-light, they having then as well as by day, a little Advanc'd-guard, and there ought to be plac'd between it and them Sentinels on Horse-back, with Orders to listen very attentively to hear what passes, and upon all occasions to give notice of what they hear, to the Guard ; he that commands this little Guard is to inform the Commander of the great Guard, and he the Person who commands the General of the Horse's Guard. Some Officers to ease their Men and their Horses keep but one

Rank

Rank on Horfeback to be relieved every hour; but this ought not to be done, efpecially if the Enemy be near, but he that commands the little advance Guard ought to fuffer none of his Men to alight, The Sentinels which are plac'd in the Night ought to be double, for being Two together, they will not be fo apt to fall afleep; they are relieved from hour to hour; but before they are allowed to joyn the Squadron, they are obliged to go upon the Patrole, having a Word and a Signal given to them, that there may be no diforder when they meet; there happen very nice affairs fometimes to the Officers upon the Guard: For I have known in *Flanders* Sentinels defert to go into the Enemies Army, which was within a quarter of a League of ours; upon this occafion the Word which is given, muft be chang'd, and the General of the

Horfe

Horse acquainted with the deser-
tion, for then is the greatest like-
lihood of being attacqued by the
Enemy, they thinking to gain great
advantage by the Word, being
discover'd to them by the deserter.
This caution must be used also
when they take Prisoners, any of
those which are upon the Patrole,
lest they learn from them the
Word, and then endeavour to surprize you: An Officer which commands the Guard, ought always
to be on Horseback, and every
quarter of an hour visit his advanc'd Corps-de guard, and his
Sentinels, but if he be not able to
watch himself, he must desire the
Officer which commands next to
him, to have an Eye to every thing,
and to awaken him, if any thing
happens. It is commonly at the
break of day, that the Enemy makes
any attempt; and then we are to
send the General notice, so soon as

I　　　　any

any thing appears, but we ought
not to quit our Posts, how eager
soever we may be to fight, for a
Guard is set only for the security
of the Camp, and unless it be attacqued, it is to shew one does
not know ones business to come to
blows; but however, if the Enemy
charges any small Guard, which is
a detachment of that which one
commands, a Man ought to fly
to its assistance; the reason of this
is, because we our selves are attacqued when those Posts are, which
we are to keep; but when there
are two small Corps de guard detach'd from the Main-guard, and
that the one is attacqued, the
other ought notwithstanding not
to stir, for it would be to be feared, that whilst that is imployed in
yielding succours to the other, the
Enemy would endeavour to gain
their Post; they ought therefore to
wait the Orders of the Commander

der in chief of the Great Guard,
who is to determin what they are
to do.

As there is moft commonly more
than one Guard fet for the fafety
of the Army, fo if one be attacqued, it is not for the others to
run to their affiftance, without being commanded, for the reafon I
have already given. It is the fame
thing when an alarm is taken, for
although every one is obliged to
make ready, and ftand at their
Arms at the head of the Camp;
yet they muft not run every where,
where they hear Action; their
Courage muft not tranfport them
fo as to march without Order,
and we acquit our felves beft of
our Duty, when we are ready to
do, what we receive command to
do. The Kings Guards did not
heretofore Mount the Guard of
the Camp, but at prefent they are
no more exempted than others;

their

their reafons for it, were that they were to be upon no Guard of Fatigue: but it being that which accuftoms our bodies to War, the King has ordered they fhall do the fame Duty as his other Forces do when the Enemies appear, and the General refolves to Engage them; the Guard may demand it as their right to be plac'd in the Front of the Battel; this Guard is relieved every 24 hours, and the Officer which relieves it, has always his Sword drawn, and takes the right hand of the Perfon he relieves.

As to the *Piquet*; it is a detachment of Men, who are always near the General, ready to execute whatfoever he commands them; wherefore they are always Booted, and their Horfes Sadled; they are very ufeful in an Army, for alarms may happen to be given at all times, and thefe Men are always
ready

ready to go where there is need of them; so that a General cannot then be surprized, their imployment in the day of decampment is to take care of the ways, and to see them mended, that the march of the Army may not be retarded. The Kings Guards seldom furnish Men to do this Duty, but sometimes they do.

The Guard of the Colours, is that which is drawn out of each Regiment of Horse, to guard the Colours which are at the head of the Camp, they ought to be booted, and their Swords drawn when they are upon Duty, altho they are on Foot. The Kings Guards do this Duty as well as others, and it is upon this Duty the Officers put those who have committed any fault, which is a great mortifica-tion to them, being seen and known by all that pass by. It is the Duty of this Guard to watch that there

be

be no immoralities committed in the Nigh time in the Regiment; they are alfo refponfible for any thing that is loft in the Night-time, therefore it behoves the Officer that commands it not to negle&t his Duty. The Colonel commonly fets near his Tent a Sentinel taken from this Guard, who is relieved every hour, this he does by his own Authority, and is authorized to do it by Cuftom.

The Orderly Guard is a detachment, which is made out of every Regiment of Horfe, of Men who go to the General of the Horfe his Tent, and remain there to receive Orders; fothat if there happens any thing that requires haft, they are fent to theirrefpective Regiments, whereby they are all able to put themfelves in a readinefs at the fame inftant of time: The Kings Guards are equally obliged with the reft, to furnifh
Men

Men for this Duty, but with this distinction, that they are always lookt upon as Officers, and admitted to the General of the Horse his Table; but I have known the time when they were no more lookt upon, than other private Sentinels, which was in 1667. and then they were often commanded by a Corporal of Light-horse, they being detach'd without distinction with them.

The Generals Guard, is only to honour his Charracter, it confisting but of Foot, which is always commanded by a Captain. The Lieutenant Generals and the Marshals *de Camp*, have always Guards, but they are only mounted by inferior Officers: The Kings Guards are never upon the Guard, but to His Majesty, and there is then always both Horse and Foot. The Officer of the Generals Guard, eats always at his Table, where let the throng

I 4 . be

be never fo great, there is a place left for him: This Guard is mounted by turns, as all others are, and is relieved every 24 hours.

The great Guard and the ordinary Guard, are thofe which are fubfervient to the Guard of the Camp, which is call'd the great Guard, and is mounted by whole Regiments, or half Regiments. The great Guard, and the ordinary Guard, have different Pofts in the Day-time, but they draw together at Night; and then, if there be no Colonel nor Major prefent, the eldeft Captain commands both. A Soldier that deferts when he is upon the Guard or ftands Sentinel, endeavouring to get to the Enemy, is much more feverely punifhed if he is caught, then if he had taken another time to run away, for they are not fhot to Death, but hang'd. Thofe alfo are hang'd who go to the Enemies, altho

altho they are not upon the Guard,
but moft commonly, thofe who
defert being upon the Guard, or
ftanding Sentinel are punifh'd with
much more feverity than the others.
At *Lifle*, I faw a *Switzer* for this
Crime condemn'd, firft to lofe his
Ears and his Nofe, and then to be
hang'd. I have feen others made
to run the Gantlet before they
were hang'd: The punifhment of
running the Gantlet is very fevere,
it being executed in the manner
following. There is a lane made
by the Regiment, the Criminal being forc'd to run through it with
his fhoulders bare, and every Soldier having in his hand a hazle
fwitch which will not break, the
Soldiers being obliged not to favour him ; for if they are difcover'd
to do fo by their Officer, they are
feverely punifh'd; the Criminal
fometimes is forc'd to take two or
three turns in this manner, till the

I 5   blood.

blood gushes out from his shoulders on all sides; this is the difference which I have observed to be made between the punishment of a Man, who deserts being upon the Guard, or upon Duty, and that inflicted upon one who deserts in a Garison, or in the Army; but they are all punish'd with Death, if they are taken going to the Enemy. It seems to me that *Soldiers* have imitated in these sorts of punishments the common Judges; for we see that when a Man is Guilty of a very great Crime, they sentence his Hand to be cut off, before he is Executed. I have said that all are to be hang'd, taken going to the Enemy; and I saw a memorable Example of this in the first *Dutch* Campaign; for a Captain in an *Italian* Regiment, being taken running away into *Holland*, was together with all his Soldiers hang'd upon one Gallows at *Emerick*.

There

There is also another Guard which is call'd the *Bivac*, which is only used in Sieges; and when the Enemies are very strong or near to us, none are exempted from this, and the whole Army mounts it together, or half of it, according to the occasion: It is not to be relieved every 24 hours, for they mount it at Night, and go off in the Morning, this is done very exactly, till there are lines of Circumvallation made, which when finished, they give themselves more rest, there not being need of so many upon this Guard.

An Officer who desires to know what these Guards are, must be on Horseback every day, and be where they are drawn together, where he will find most part of the Officers of the Army; *viz.* The Generals of the Horse, the Brigadiers, the Colonels, and sometimes the Lieutenant General, and the

Marshal

Marshals *de Camp*; he ought to follow the great Guard one day, and
another the ordinary Guard, to see
how they mount them, and how
they come off from them, that he
may know his Duty when it comes
to his turn; when an Officer is
commanded to the ordinary Guard,
he must command the Men of his
Regiment together, to the head of
the Camp, half an hour before the
time prefixed, and march them to
the Parade place, to the end that
the General of Horse may find you
there, and take notice of your exactness in the discharge of your Duty; and besides it being much fitter
you should wait for him, than he
for you, by taking care not to fail
in little things of this nature, you
will soon gain the Reputation of
being a good Officer; for your
shewing an exactness in the difcharge of your Duty, is of more
advantage than all you can do in

a

a Fight; befides, there are every
day to be found Men of Courage,
and who behave themfelves well,
but not fuch as will make it their
whole bufinefs to caufe the Kings
fervice to be well done by others:
when our Officer therefore is detach'd upon any fervice, he ought
always to be the firft at his Arms;
for the Soldiers taking Example by
him, will ufe their endeavours to
perform their Duty well, when they
are fatisfi'd he does his. They are
very fevere judges of all our Actions, and if we difcover any want,
either of Courage or Conduct, they
are the firft to cenfure us amongft
themfelves; therefore a Man for
his own Reputation and Honour,
muft be very exact when the Kings
fervice requires it, and not over-
look any fault; but when an
Officer is not upon Duty, he may
ufe them with more mildnefs, for
he is able, if they make an ill ufe
of

of it, foon to bring them back to
their Duty. But in all the experience I have had, I have always
found mildnefs prevail more with
them, than feverity, and that they
have never made an ill ufe of my
civility to them.

An Officer ought never to fuffer
his Men to Rob, without punifhing
them feverely for it; and as foon as
any complaints are made to him,
or any thing of this nature comes
to his knowledge, he ought to
make a publick Example of the
offenders, yet he may order it fo,
as to fpare the them confufion of con-
feffing their Crime; and I have
very often caufed what was ftoln,
to be reftored without letting any
body know who ftole it, nor did
I know my felf; for I commanded
that in marching, they fhould let
fall what was ftoln; and they ftood
in fuch fear of me, that the Perfon
injur'd, immediately found what
                                    he

he had loft, in the Rear of the Squadrons; this does efpecially amongft Horfe, for they ftand more upon point of Honour, than the Foot; and indeed they are treated after much another rate than the Foot; for they are corrected with the Cane, but that is never done to the others, or at leaft ought not. A private Sentinel of the Regiment of St. *Aouft*, having been beaten with a ftick by his Officer, and having complained to the General, the General reproved the Officer feverely, and commanded him to ufe his Men more civilly for the future, the order is to Correct them with the flat of the Sword; but I would have even this ufed as little as may be, for a Man who has any Honour, does not eafily bear blows, which is often the caufe of their deferting. The King once told Monfieur *Chazeron* Lieutenant of the Guards *de Corps,*
who

who complained to him, that he
was forced to be always beating
of them, to make them obey; as
for me, if I were in your place
I had rather kill them, than beat
them; for if you beat them,
you cannot be beloved by them.
I never mifufed any of my Troop
in my life, and yet excepting twice,
I always made that to be reftored
which they had taken; it is much
harder to make them reftore what
they have taken, than to be obeyed
in any thing elfe; and tho they
did difobey me in this point twice,
yet they got nothing by their theft,
they apprehended my anger fo
much. The firft time that this
hapned to me, was at *Roie*; where
having my Quarters at the *Sara-
cens-Head*, they took a pair of
Sheets, in which my Servants had
lain, and the Landlord having made
his Complaint to me; I promifed
him either to caufe them to be reftored.

stored to him, or to pay him for
them; and having declar'd I would
have them found again, I commanded that the Person who had
taken them, should hide them in
my Stable, where he hid them in
the Rack, covering them with Hay;
when my Troop was together, I
renew'd the command in General,
which I had given to every one in
particular; but finding this did no
good, I marched out of the Town,
and commanded them in the presence of my Landlord, desiring
him to go with me, to let the Sheets
drop as they had done many things
before; but finding that this also
was to no purpose, I was forc'd
to search their Bags, and to unsad-
dle their Horses, they often hiding
what they steal under their Sad-
dles, but what I lookt for, could
not be found; so that I was forc'd
to pay my Landlord for his Sheets,
who restored me the Money a year
af-

afterwards, telling me where he had found them. This Example suffices to prove that blows are not always neceſſary to make an Officer be obeyed, but that there is another way of making himſelf fear'd. The ſecond time that I could not make them reſtore what they had ſtoln, was in a Village of *Alſatia*, upon the Frontier of *Lorain*, the Army was then retiring into their Winter Quarters, and it being towards the latter ſeaſon of the year, the Forces were cantoniſed, one Regiment on one ſide of the Country, and another on the other, *&c.* There was no Captain but was lodged under cover, and a Houſe falling to my ſhare, I allowed Fourteen of my Troop, for whom I had ſomething of conſideration, and I thought were honeſt Gentlemen, to Lodge in the houſe with me, yet notwithſtanding next morning there was a complaint
made

made of a pair of Sheets loft, and not
being able to make them reftore
them, every one juftifying himfelf, that he had not taken them, I
was forc'd to pay for them, as I
had done for the others; but not
being willing to ufe them to play
me fuch tricks too often, I ftopt
out of the pay of every one, as much
as I had given to the Peafant out of
whofe houfe they were loft, of
which they complained; faying,
that all I could pretend to, was
to have enough to reimburfe my
felf from them all; but having anfwer'd them, that if they would
difcover to me the Perfon who had
done the Fact, I would ftop it out
of his pay only; they rather chufe
to lofe their Money, than to make
any difcovery of one another: I
have fince heard, that they had
hidden the Sheets in fome part of
the houfe, fearing a fearch; however, this action was not difappro-
ved

ved by any who came to the knowledge of it ; and which is more, my Men never returned to commit the same fault again, or at least I had never any complaint made to me , nor no such thing at least ever came to my knowledge.

In my opinion, an Officer cannot do himself more right than at first, when he enters into service, to shew his aversion to these Robberies , and to be severe in the punishing of them , this keeps a Soldier in awe, and tho he be never so much inclined to thievry, he will do it in fear, knowing his Officers humor, is not to suffer it ; there are Officers who do not approve of this maxim, thinking they cannot have a good Troop, if they do not give them some liberty of this kind ; but this ought to be done with this distinction, that when they are in an Enemies Country, tty, they may be permitted many things, but that every where else an Officer is answerable, before God and Man, for all the Robberies which he suffers them to commit, who are under his command. A Captain who had been long in the War, and who was a Man of great honour and honesty; being asked by some others who were less scrupulous than he was, why he would not suffer his Soldiers to take so much as a Hen; 'tis answer'd he, because I have sins enough of my own, without bringing upon me the sins of others; and indeed a Captain who suffers the Widow and Orphan to be dispoyled, is bound to make Restitution, either in this life, or the next, altho he had no share in the profit of the Robbery. The Prince of *Conty*, who has made himself admired by all *France* for his holy Conversion, was so sensible of the

in·

indifpenfiblenefs of this obligation, that being willing to repair the loffes, which the Country had fuftein'd by the Army, which he Commanded in *Catalonia* in his Life-time, fent Servants on purpofe to all places where he had Quartered, to inform themfelves what every one had fuffer'd; and upon their report to him, he order'd them to be reimburft: There cannot be too much caution ufed in in a thing whereon fo much depends our Salvation; and befides, as I have already faid, there is no body, whatfoever fhew he may make, that he does not apprehend the Judgments of God, but does when he knows he has juftly curr'd his difpleafure; wherefore it is an Officers intereft, to preferve his Soldiers in their innocency, for when they are laden with Crimes, they will go into the Battel, but with trembling; he ought to overcome

come or die with them; and what affiftance is there to be expected from Men, who tremble even before they fee the faces of their Enemies?

CHAP. XIV.

How an Officer is to behave himfelf, if a Command be given to another, which is due to him, or when he is commanded out of his place.

IN War, Commands are of different kinds; in fome there is Honour to be acquir'd; in others, according to all likelyhood, there is nothing but trouble; thefe are avoided as much as may be, and no body loves to go upon thefe Duties out of his place; but the others are fought after with eager-nefs, not grudging to be always on Horfeback upon fuch an ac-

count

count: yet if an Officer be commanded out of his place upon a troublefom Duty, he ought notwithftanding, to obey, the Kings fervice not admitting of any delay or difpute that which he may do, when he comes back, is to make his complaint, and then he is reproved who commanded him without having reafon for what he did.

But I would not advife a young Man to trouble his Officers with fuch a complaint, if it has hapned but once to him; efpecially, a young Man, who ought always to be ready for all fervice; otherwife he will be fufpected of Lazinefs, and unlefs he perceives, that they take pleafure in playing him often thefe tricks, he ought to content himfelf with telling the Perfon who fends him, that unlefs he will take care to fee the Duty done by every one in his turn, he will complain to his Colonel, as to the com-

commands of honour; they cannot be taken from us without doing us a great prejudice, wherefore an Officer ought not to remain filent, when an Aid-Major who knows it is our right to March, commands another in our place; there muft then complaint be made, and Juftice is always done to us, and he receives a reprimand, if the fault be his; but fometimes there is an exprefs order from the General to caufe another to March in our place: a Man is very unhappy when this happens, and it is a mark of the fmall accompt which is made of us, but it's to be confider'd that if he who is commanded is a common Party-man, we receive no prejudice by it, for it is the cuftom now to chufe thofe perfons *preferably to* all others; *La Fite* Lieutenant of the Guards *du Corps*, St. *Silveftre*, *Melac*, Colonels of the Horfe, and fome other

K **Officers**

Officers are detach'd every day out of their places, to go upon parties and no body takes it ill, becaufe making that their profeffion, they are fuppofed to know it better than any others, it is free for any one to follow their Example, and to eftablifh himfelf upon the fame foot, but in my opinion it is a very nice profeffion; for befides that, there is required a great fhare of Wifdom and Conduct, it is alfo neceffary to be lucky, for a Party-man is more efteem'd for the fuccefs he has in his enterprifes, than for the caution he ufes. *Vignol*, a Captain in the Commiffary Regiment was brought into great Credit for two Actions; the fuccefs of both which he ow'd more to Fortune, than to his own Conduct; not that I will fay, but that he is a brave Man, and very capable of managing an enterprife; but I leave it to the World to judge, whether all the World

World would not have done the same as he did, in both the occasions which I am going to relate.

After the taking of *Limburgh*, the King having detach'd several Officers to get some intelligence of the Enemy, sent him out four or five Leagues round about the Army: in his return, he met with a party of about 100 Horse of the Enemy, who had taken five and twenty or thirty of the Kings Guards, and were carrying them away into their Camp; at the sight of which, he was so moved, that he charged them desperately, and after having put them to flight, he released the Prisoners, who during the Fight, did on their parts all that was in their power to make him come off with honour. Another time being out upon a party towars *Mons*, there came a party of the Enemies to put themselves in Ambuscade in the same place

K 2   where

where he was, and he who commanded them not knowing his businefs, went into it without difcovering the place, but *Vignols* falling upon him unawars beat him, and took a great many who were prifoners, which he carried away with him to the Camp, where this ftill raifed his Reputation higher, which was already eftablifh'd by the Action I related concerning the Guards. I leave it to the World to Judge as I faid before, if in either of thefe Actions there did not appear to be as much luck as Conduct or Prudence; however, I fay not this to take from his Reputation, I know he is a Man very brave in his Perfon, and has given many other marks of it befides thefe; and particularly in the encounter he had with the Count *de Stirum*, a near Kinfman to the Prince of *Orange* in the firft *Dutch* Campaign; for he defended himfelf againft 500 Horfe,

Horfe, for three whole hours in an Old houfe, although he was not near fo ftrong as the Enemy: at length the Enemy having fet it on Fire, he fallied out like a Lion at the head of 15 or 20 ftout Men, and having met with the Count *de Stirum*, who endeavour'd to obftruct his paffage, he kill'd him with his own hand, and would not yield himfelf, till after he had feen all his own party either kill'd or difabl'd for fight.

But to come back to my Subject: I fay therefore that a Man may at any time when he pleafes put himfelf upon the Foot of a Party-man, but I never could find there was much honour to be gained by it, nor any great Fortune to be made, unlefs a Man be very lucky; for a General efteems them but according to the number of Prifoners they bring, and the ufe they are of to him; otherwife they be-

come

come objects of scorn and laughter;
but however, a Man that desires
to advance himself in a short time,
ought not to be disgusted with all
these difficulties; for a Man may
hope to carry his Fortune very
far if he succeeds in this, and it is
always a certain way to make ones
self known; for his profession being
that of an adventure, he ought to
trust Fortune to a great degree,
but it is necessary for him to fight,
whether he be strongest or weakest,
for he will be laughed at by every
one, if he lets the Enemy escape
without charging them. I know
a Person who is now a great Man,
who for not having followed this
Rule, suffer'd some jeers at his coming first into the service; he had
been out upon two or three parties
without doing any thing; and being upon the same Duty a fourth
time, having met with the Enemy
who was much stronger than he,

he

he retreated into the Woods, and
sent to desire Monsieur *de Turene*
to send him some Foot to make
good his Retreat; but Monsieur *de
Turene* returned him for answer,
that a Man who was at the head
of a commanded Party, ought never to demand succours, especially
since he had been out three times
already without drawing his Sword;
that he might do what he pleased,
but he had none to send him. He
that charges first in the Night-time,
has always the better of it, for the
darkness hindering the Enemy from
knowing what number he has with
him, always takes him to be stronger than he is; he must always take
care when he meets another Party
abroad, not to be prevailed upon
by fair words; for oftentimes Men
when they find themselves the weaker Party, will say they are of the
same Army, and so escape out of
the hands of their Enemy, taking

ad-

advantage of our eafinefs of belief; therefore though a Troop fhould at firft fay they are of the fame Party, an Officer notwithftanding ought ftill to remain upon his Guard, until they have fully prov'd that what they fay is true ; the Proverb being very true, that miftruft is the mother of fafety. In 1668. a little before the Treaty of *Aix la Chapelle*, an Officer in the Royal forreign Regiment, being fent out with 40 Horfe, and the Scouts having met with thofe of the Enemies, who being asked who they were for, anfwer'd *France*; which our Scouts believing, did let fall their Arms, and began to mix with them, as if they had been their Friends and Country-men; our whole Troop when come up, did the fame ; but the Enemy ftill having their Carbines ready, fir'd upon them, when they leaft fufpected it; and having kill'd a good
many

many of them made the reft Prifoners; the Enemies party was a detachment out of Monfieur *de Louvignies* Regiment, who has fince
Commanded the *Ofnabruk* Forces,
and is at prefent Governour of *Mef-
fina*; this Colonel having upon all
occafions fhew'd the Count *de Roie*,
the great defire he had to oblige him,
did fo in this, fending him back all
the Prifoners without Ranfom; they
always ufe this civility to each o-
ther, for their having once met in
fervice caufed this great dear-
nefs between them; their acquain-
tance began in this manner: When
Monfieur *de Turene* fent out a detachment to inveft *Ypres*, before
the *Pyrenean* treaty, the Enemies
preft fo hard the Front of this detachment, that the firft Squadrons
broke in upon thofe which follow-
lowed. The Count *de Roie*, who
Commanded the Rear-guard, was
pofted in a ditch at the head of his

Regiment, and fearing that the
runaways might caufe a diforder
in his Ranks he let them pafs, which
when they had done, he made good
his ground againft the Enemies,
who purfued ours with great eager-
nefs. Monfieur *Louvignies*, who
led up the *Spaniards* to the charge,
feeing the refolute countenance of
Monfieur *de Roie*, ftopt fhort, to
let his Men take breath, and to give
them time to draw together; they
had both their Piftols drawn, and
fir'd almoft upon each other at the
fame time, and were both wounded,
the one in the Arm, and the other
in the Thigh; but Monfieur *Louvignies*'s wound, they fay was given
him by a private Soldier; after this
the Troops charged each other, and
the *Spaniards* not being able to
withftand the fhock, were forc'd
to retreat as faft as they had purfued; this Action had bred as I
have faid, a reciprocal efteem in
these

thefe two Officers, fo that fince
that time they never let any opportunity flip of fhewing it to each
other.

This Example fhews plainly e-
nough, that an Officer ought always to be upon his Guard, and
not of too eafie belief; for miftruft
puts a Man out of danger of any
furprize; wherefore when he meets
with a Troop, he muft not immediately return his Arms, becaufe
they fay they are of the fame fide,
but examin them ftrictly of what
Regiment, the names of their Officers, and put Queftions enough
to them to find out the truth. There
are fome who make ufe of the Pafs-
ports of others, to effect their defigns; this is a very cunning artifice,
and a Man muft take a great deal
of care not to be cheated by it;
for a Pafsport may be fallen into
the hands of the Enemy, and who
knows but he will make ufe of
it

it to entrap thofe he hath to deal with; the following Example will fhew that the thing is not impoſſible, and upon the Relation that I ſhall make, I leave it to every one to take his meaſures. A Lieutenant in the Regiment of the *Switzers*, which was engariſon'd at *Maſtricht*, having been detach'd in the year 1675. to go upon a Party, met with one ſent out by the Enemy, which he put to flight after having kill'd the Commander, amongſt the papers which were found upon the dead Man, they brought him a Paſsport, which putting in his Pocket without thinking it could be any uſe to him; he went to put himſelf in Ambuſcade in another place, but as he marched, he met with a Party of Horſe of the Gariſon of *Luxenburgh*, and ſeeing himſelf the weakeſt, was forc'd to make uſe of a Stratagem, and ſay he was of the

ſame

same side, shewing the Passport which he had in his Pocket. The Officer who Commanded the Enemies believed it to be true, and remaining without suspition returned his Arms, so that they continued marching together like good friends, and went into a Village where the Officer of Horse intended to bait; he put all his Horses into a Church-yard, and after having set his Sentinels, went with the greatest part of his Men into a Cabaret to Dinner, as if he had been in no danger; but the *Switzer* thinking this time very seasonable for him to do what he design'd, left some of his Men in the Church-yeard, to seize and lead away the Horses, and went with the rest of them, and finding the Officer, and his Men at Dinner, he took them all Prisoners, they making no resistance; so the *Switzer* brought back to *Maſtricht* a

great

the reason is, that when they go
so far off, they are commonly but
few in number, as five, seven or
nine; and then they will be taken
rather, for people got together to
rob than for fair Enemies.

But not to make a longer digreſſion, I ſay that the ſending
out a Man which is uſed to it,
upon a party, is of no prejudice
to us, although it ſhould be our
turn to march. Excepting in which
caſe it is not to be done; for it is
to have very little confidence in
a Man, to give a Command which
is due to him, to another; but yet
even this is not without Example,
and I ſhall here take notice of what
is to be done upon ſuch an occaſion. When Monſieur *de Rochfort*
was before *Maſtricht*, in the year
1672. he detach'd Monſieur *de
Lanſon* Lieutenant of the Guards
du Corps, with 200 Horſe of the
Kings Guards, to guard a Million
of

great many Horses and Prisoners, and every one having known in what manner he had behaved himself, esteemed him the more.

Troops which are in Garison, and go out upon parties for many days take always a Pasport, for without one, they would be taken for Robbers; these Passes are limited to a certain day, and when that time is expired, they must come back to renew them, unless they will run the venture of being hang'd, for if they fall into the hands of the Enemy; they are not lookt upon as Soldiers, but as a company of dissolute people who make use of that Character, only to commit Robbery and Spoil. As to the parties which are sent out from the Army, they do not stand in need of Passes, unless they go very far into the Enemies Country; and then they are as necessary for them, as if they were Garison Forces;
the

of Livers which was at *Sedan,* and
the Army had need of, who furprized in the middle of his way a
party of the Enemies which was
baiting in a Village, and having
learnt from the Peafants, that one
half of the party was in a neighbouring wood, he fet two little
parties on the skirts of it, to purfue them if they came out; thefe
two little parties were made up,
the one out of the Guards *du Corps,*
the other of Gendarms, Lighthorfe; and Musktteers, the Command of the firft belonged to the
eldeft of the Life Guard, and the
other to the eldeft Gendarm; but
the looks of the Gendarm, not being
liked by Monfieur *de Lanfon*, he
asked to fee another, and he pleafing
him no better, he gave the Command to a Light-horfeman, commanding the reft to obey him;
that which thefe two Gendarms, to
whom this injuftice was fhewn,

were

were to have done, was to retire from the service, and so ought all of the same body to have done; for it being their right to Command the Light horse, this affront was done to them all, and if they had complained, Monsieur *de Lanson* could not have made any excuse, but would have been reprov'd for it by the General.

The following Example is more nice, and it is thought a Man cannot at such a time exempt himself from receiving orders, from the person whom by right he ought to Command. At the Siege of *Maſtricht*, the Cornet of the Commiſſary Regiment, of whom I have formerly spoken, having been detach'd upon an Advance-Guard to beat back the Enemy, who had been Foraging in the Corn-fields, and acquitted him so well of this Duty, that the King commanded him to be the next day upon the

Guard

Guard at the same Post; commanding a Lieutenant, who was to be there for his assistance to obey him; this command surpriz'd every body, there having seldom been any of the like nature given, which caused a great deal of discourse amongst the Officers; who having well weigh'd every thing, all agreed that the Lieutenant did well in obeying; it being lawful for the King, or even a General to change the Oeconomy of things, but not for any other Officer, who is responsible himself for what he does.

CHAP.

CHAP. XV.

Of Parties, and of the measures they are to take.

Since I have spoken in the foregoing Chapter of Parties, I shall here finish my Relation with what I have observed concerning them: To do this Duty well, it is absolutely necessary to know the Country, and where Ambuscades may be laid, for when they have need of a Guide to shew them; they run a great risque of being beaten; a Guide being commonly of the Country where the seat of the War is; and what trust is there to be put in a Man, who sees all his Country-men and friends ruined, and brought into despair? For is it not most likely, that if it were in his power, he would have

the

the whole Army beaten, to deliver his Country from the miseries which are caused by their remaining in it; besides when the Commander of a party is upon the March, he ought never to go the direct way, but skirt of each side of him, to take from the Enemy any knowledge of the way he marches; for it is always to be supposed the Enemy has Scouts out in the Country, therefore we ought to use as much caution as if we were pursued; an Ambuscade ought never to be laid in the night before having well examined the place, otherwise they would be exposed to the inconveniencies I have before observed, in speaking of *Vignoles*. The Sentinels must be so plac'd, that they may not be discover'd by the Enemy, and they ought always to be set double. The Sentinels ought never to be suffer'd to alight, although I have

known

known some Officers maintain it
to be better to have the Sentinels
on foot, because being so, they may
lay their ears to the ground, and
thereby sooner discover than by
trusting to their Eyes, if there be
any Enemies abroad; but in this
case there is but one allowed to
alight, but in my opinion it is
much better to keep to the ancient
rule; which is, that a Sentinel
ought not to alight upon any occasion whatsoever; and as for the
rest of the party, if it be Horse,
the Commander ought not to suffer
any of by them to alight, for if
the Enemy should come upon them,
there would be too much time
required for them to mount their
Horses; and besides, it is to be
fear'd, it cannot be done without
noise, and giving such warning to
the Enemy, as will give them leisure
to go too far for you to overtake
them; if it is Foot, they ought always

ways to be at their Arms, for if
the Soldiers be allowed to rest
themselves, they will be sure to
sleep; and when 'tis necessary for
them to Fight, it will be very hard
to awaken them; which when they
are on a sudden, they are most in-
clinable to fear. Stone-Horses are
very unfit for going upon a party,
for it being absolutely necessary,
that an Enemy should not discover
the Ambuscade which is laid for
him; the neighing of a Horse may
give them notice of what we would
not have them know. It is related
in a famous Author, that *Darius*
was chosen King, for the neighing
of his Horse; but in this case on
the contrary, instead of being an
advantage to a Man, it may often
cost him his Life. This History
being a very pleasant one, I have
thought it would not be disagree-
able to the Reader to relate it;
after the *Magicians* had taken away
the

the Crown of *Perfia*, from the family of *Cyrus*, the great Men of the Kingdom assembled themselves as well to punish these offenders, as to make election of one to succeed him; but instead of agreeing in the choice of the person, every one pretended to the Crown himself, which had threatned the State with a civil War; had not the most Judicious amongst them, to prevent a civil War proposed this expedient, *viz.* that they should assemble themselves in a certain place, and that he whose Horse did first neigh, should be acknowledged King by the rest; and this agreement being published in the Town, a Groom belonging to *Darius*, who wisht his Master might have the Crown, led in the Night-time the Horse which *Darius* was accustom'd to ride, to the place appointed, and there letting him smell to a Mare, the Horse neighed all the while he was there;
the

and the Groom continued this trick
until the day appointed came; at
which time, the great Men being
affembl'd, when *Darius* entred the
place, his Horfe remembring what
had hapned to him, began to neigh,
fo that the great Men of the Kingdom to comply with their engage-
ment, acknowledged *Darius* for
their King; but the cafe is quite
different with us, for whereas, it
was of importance for him, for his
Horfe to neigh for the gaining of
a Crown; it no lefs imports us that
our Horfe fhould forbear, left it
make us lofe both Life and Reputation.

An Officer muft himfelf keep
great filence, and fee it alfo kept
by all his Men, when he is in Ambufcade, it being his Duty to go
from time to time between the ranks
to keep every one awake; Scouts
muft not be fent out in the night,
but always as foon as day breaks,
before

before the Ambufcade be raifed, which is commonly done before the Sun appears, unlefs there be an order to the contrary, or that they are of fuch ftrength as not to apprehend any thing; the reafon of this is, that if they ftayed longer, ther the Enemy would certainly have notice of it; and it may be, cut them off in their Retreat: A Man ought never to make his Retreat by the fame way he came, becaufe the Enemy knowing there is a party abroad will make a ftronger detachment than he has with him, and charge them in his Retreat; therefore to put them out in their meafures it is beft never to Retreat the fame way one came. There is great caution to be ufed in ones march, till arrived in the Camp; for if as I have faid, the Enemy places often their Ambufcade at the Gates of a Town, they do it alfo often at the entry of a

L   Camp,

Camp, always thinking its nearness will make an Officer less mindfull of his Duty. When an Officer has orders to get intelligence at any rate, he must seize upon the first person he meets, but otherwise it would not be worth his while to discover himself, for the taking of one two or three persons; for then it would be said of him, that he went out, and returned without running any hazard, for the Enemy must be more numerous than we are to gain any Reputation by them, and some blood must be shed. I do not mean but that they may discover themselves to take some small party, but that which is done in this case, commonly is that after having made them Prisoners, contenting themselves with keeping them, they wait for a more favourable opportunity to gain honour. Men in an Ambuscade ought never to dis-

cover

cover themfelves till the Enemy is
fo near, that he cannot efcape;
for if a Man fhould do fo, fo foon
as he fees the Enemy, he will run
the cenfure of being thought to
have no mind to Fight. An Officer of the Gendarms more confiderable for his Birth and Command,
than for the Reputation he had
gotten in the War; having often
perfecuted the General to fend him
out, with a party of commanded
Men, obtained of him by being
importunate what would not have
been granted to him, either for his
Courage or Conduct; and his command requiring that he fhould not
march at the head of a fmall party,
he had 400 Horfe given to him,
with which he put himfelf in Ambufcade in a place where he could
not fail in a fhort time of feeing
the Enemy; and in effect, they
appeared in a few hours; the Sentinel informing this new Officer of

it, but withal, that they were yet at a very great diftance; yet notwithftanding this, he prefently difcovered himfelf with all his Men, which forc'd the Enemy to face about, who being noar half a Miles diftance from him, faved themfelves in the Woods before he could come to them. I do really think the Officer intended to do his beft, and would have been very glad to have fignalized himfelf; but however, whether what he did, was out of want of experience, or what was imputed to him by others, *viz.* that he was glad to avoid fighting; the King was no fooner informed of the affair, but he ordered him to fell his command. In the *Dutch* Campaign Colonel *Maffiette*, a *Flemifh* Gentleman, an Officer of great Reputation amongft the *Spaniards*, in whofe fervice he had been a long time, undertook to furprize and take Prifoners the

ad-

advanced Guard of our Army; in order to which, he laid himself in Ambuscade in a neighbouring wood, and taking the time when they had unbridled, he charged them with so much mettle, that he put the greatest part of them to flight, there being only the Marquess of *Montgomery*, who was ashamed to run away, who resisted *Massiette* to the utmost of his power, but very few came in to his assistance, and afterwards his Horse being kill'd, he was at last forc'd to yield himself up Prisoner to the Enemy. The King being immediately informed of the brave resistance he had made, commended him in the presence of all his Officers, and blamed very much those who had been so base as to run away, giving orders that all should be cashier'd who were attainted or convicted of Cowardize, in this Action: The next day the King

L 3   going

going to view a Castle which was
within Musket-shot of the high-
way, he perceived three Men coming out of the Enemies Quarters,
which he presently found to be
Prisoners sent back by *Massiette*
upon their Paroles ; amongst which
was the Marquess of *Montgomery*
which made him stop, and embracing him, assured him he would
take care of him; and to shew
how pleasing his services had been
to him, he might assure himself he
should have the command of the
first Regiment that fell in the Army, and that for the Horse that
had been kill'd in fighting for him,
he would give him another as good,
which he performed immediately,
by giving him one of the best
which was in his own Stable, and
the command of a Regiment as he
had promised.

To

To come back then to my Subject, I dare maintain that all thofe
who would be efteem'd skilfull
Men upon a party, muft always
bring Prifoners home ; for they will
foon be laughed at, if they go out
only to beat the Fields; as for me,
I look upon it that it is better upon thefe occafions, to have a few
with one than many : The reafon
is , that a great number cannot
march without being feen, whereas
with a little one, it is much eafier
to conceal a march , befides not
difcovering themfelves, but when
they pleafe they take their time fo
well as never to do it to no purpofe ;
and befides all that , if they are
purfued, their Retreat is much eafier, for there is much time required
in paffing a Lane, to file off and
draw up. Wherefore Monfieur
de Turene always when he had
a mind to have certain intelligence
of the Enemy, would never fend

L 4   out

out above feven Officers, an odd
number being obferved in War to
be the moft lucky, and they would
go fometimes 30 Leagues from our
Army, and would never come back
without bringing Prifoners with
them. An Officer upon thefe occafions muft carry a Carbine as
well as others; for befides the dif-
advantage there would be in having only Piftols againft Men
better Armed, he expofes himfelf
to be the firft kill'd, and by his
Death to deftroy the Party; for
the common Soldiers do not always fight out of a Principle of
honour, fo that if their Officers
were not prefent to obferve them,
they would not ftand fo firm as
they ought; it is only in the Kings
Guards that the leaft of the Officers
does not draw along with it that
of their Men, but in that body they
are almoft all capable of being fuch,
and which many of them have been,
and

and befides they all ftand upon their honour, there being fcarce any who would not rather be kill'd, than be faid to have fhewed any want of Courage in the Fight. After the Marquefs *d' Illiers* and *Chanvallon*, Officers in the Lighthorfe of the Guard, were kill'd at the Battel of *Seneffe*, the Troop notwithftanding returned to the Battel with as much refolution as before, fo that they came off with great honour; it were to be wifhed that it were the fame with the other bodies of the Army: but it having too plainly appear'd to be otherwife, it has been provided againft by placing in them at prefent, a much greater number of Officers, in proportion to what was formerly.

A Man who is detach'd with another of great Reputation, muft be fure to obferve how he behaves himfelf, for this is the only and

the

the fureft way for him to learn the
trade well; yet all Men being fubject to errors, he ought to diftin-
guifh between what is good, and
what is bad in him. I know a famous Party Commander, who when
he is not able to draw his Enemies
out of their ftrong holds, never
fails to pull down his breeches, and
fhew them his breech. This is
an Example I would not advife an
Officer to follow, it being too mean,
for there are many other ways to
fhew a Man does not fear his Enemy;
and it will be faid of an Officer
who does fuch a thing, and jufti-
fies himfelf by faying he has feen
it done by another, as it was once
of a Man who pretended to have
taken Example, by a great Author
that he has taken care to imitate
him, even in all his faults. Our
judgment ought to inform us when
he does well or ill, for experience
being not required in this cafe, a
young.

young Officer if he have sense, may know whether an old one be in the right or in the wrong, because in War all enterprises are to be grounded upon reason; for fortune ought to be trusted with the event only, it is not but some things have two handles, and which to take is often difficult to decide; because often, great praise or great blame must result from the success. There are some who hold it for a maxim, always to prefer what is safe, before what is honourable; as for me, I dare not give my judgment, but this I know, that those who succeed in following the last, get by much the greatest Reputation. It being possible that what I have related, may be difficult to be understood to some, unless they make some application of it. I shall here give another Example : When Monsieur *de Rochfort* Commanded the Kings Forces at the Blocking up of *Maestricht*; he received orders from the King to raise it, and fearing that in his Retreat, the Garison which consisted of Ten thousand Men, would set upon his Reer-guard, he commanded the whole Army to be ready to disencamp at Mid-night; and forbad the Drums to beat, or to put fire to the straw of the Camp, as is usual, lest thereby the Enemy should have notice of his design. Certainly nothing could shew more Prudence than this Command, for the Enemies were stronger than we were, altho we came to block them up; and there was reason to believe they knew their own strength, and our weakness. Yet this was not approved of by every body, and Monsieur *de Chazeron* having had orders, within two days to take the Command of those Forces, and march them towards the Marshal *de Turene*, who expected them in order

order to his march againſt the Electoror of *Brandenburg*, far from following his Example, drew up in Battalia for two hours within Cannon-ſhot of the Gariſon of *Maeſtricht*, provoking the Gariſon to ſally out by many Challenges, and ſounds of Trumpets. Theſe two ways of proceeding were very different, and yet they were both in the right. Monſieur *de Rochfort* in the condition things were in, thought it his Duty to provide for the ſafety of the Kings affairs. And it was Monſieur *de Chazeron*, on the contrary to uphold in a high meaſure the honour of his Nation, at a time eſpecially when they had done ſuch great actions, and that the Enemies were ſubdued by their loſſes. Whatever may be ſaid of theſe two actions, I dare not determine the point, it being between perſons of that great Command ; but this I cannot avoid ſaying, that

that the humour of our Nation
carrying us to approve what is
bold, and to diſlike whatſoever
looks like fear; the Action of
Monſieur *Chazerun*, had many
more admirers than that of Monſieur *de Rochfort.*

CHAP. XVI.

*How an Officer ought to behave him-
ſelf in the Fight.*

THere are two ſorts of Courage, the one which knows
no danger, and the other which
knows it, but deſpiſes it. The firſt
is call'd Fool-hardineſs, and the
other True-valour; it were to be
wiſhed that the firſt, were only poſ-
ſeſt by the common Soldier, and the
other kept in reſerve for the Officers; for they having need of judgment, for the conducting of the
others,

others, it is neceſſary for them to have the diſcretion not to engage without reaſon, nor to require any thing from them but what is feaſible, this would make an Army invincible, it having all the qualities neceſſary to carry on a Victory when there is occaſion, and to avoid Battel, when it thinks it ſelf too weak: wherefore judgment is the moſt neceſſary quallity for an Officer, that teaching him temper even in Battel; for if a Man be of a hot, paſſionate nature, what good impreſſion can he give to others, who will be apt to think that fear has produced thoſe unfortunate effects; but notwithſtanding, a Man is not to affect ſo much coldneſs, as to give any manner of cauſe to the Soldier to believe, it proceeds from any want of Courage, the Cowardize of the Officers ſoon ſhewing its effects upon the Soldiers: wherefore an Officer ought

to exhort them to do their Duty
with a pleafant countenance, and
animate them in fuch a manner,
as may fhew them, that he has
wit enough to Conduct them,
and Courage enough to fhew them
Example, he may alfo upon this
occafion loofing himfelf from his
common ferioufnefs; jeft with
them, for there is nothing which
infinuates a Man's being void of
fear, more than this humor when
he is in danger. I know one of the
greateft Men in the Kingdom, who
got great Reputation by this way,
when he firft came into the Army;
he was of a Family which was not
otherwife in any great Reputation,
for any War-like Actions; but on
the contrary, was thought to love
the Court better than the Army;
fo that he knowing the opinion
which was of it, he one day being
in the Trenches with many other
Perfons of Quality, defired them
all

all to take notice that he was the firft of his Family that ever was feen in Action, and that he would be obliged to them, if they would fend an account of it to *Mezeray,* that he might not forget to mention it in his Hiftory. I knew another in the fame place, who feeing a Soldier call'd *France,* by chance fet his Bandeleers on fire, cried out it was time to look about, fince *France* was all in a flame. Some may fay that thefe jefts may caufe a Man to be thought good Company, but not to have the more Courage; but it will be anfwer'd to him, that there are many who are of opinion, that a Man muft have a great fhare of Courage to be mafter of himfelf, to fuch a degree as to be able to be pleafant, in any great danger, it being a mark of his minds not being in the leaft difturb'd.

When

When thofe a Man charges at the head of, are ready and willing, he had better invite them to it, by difcourfe of the honour to be gained, than to terrifie them with reproaches; reproaches are good to Cowards, but Men of Courage would think it ftrange for them to be fufpected of Cowardize, when they never have given any caufe for it, either in their Actions or Words; befides which, moft Men being inclin'd to Pride, do not love to be told of their faults; it is better therefore to entertain them with the reliance a Man has upon their Courage; for they being willing to believe that what is faid of them is in earneft, moft commonly endeavour to fupport a Reputation which has coft them nothing to acquire; but if in the Battel, they fhew any mind to quit their Ranks, then all means are to be ufed, whether threats or reproaches, both
being

being very capable of making them change their minds: All Histories are full of those sorts of accidents, of which I shall here mention two Examples. In the War between *Cyrus* and *Astyages*, his Gandfather, the last perceiving that the *Medes* who had taken his part, and in whom consisted the greatest strength of his Army, and seeing them upon the point of turning their backs, commanded those in the Rear to put them all to the Sword if they stir'd; which astonished the *Medes* so much, that chusing rather to die by the hands of their Enemies, they chang'd their fear into despair, and charg'd the *Persians* who were their Antagonists, with so great a fury, that they put them all to flight. *Cyrus*, who Commanded the *Persians*, did upon this all that could be expected from a great General to rally them; but all his endeavours had been to no purpose,

had

had not their Wives, being posef-
fed with a fcorn of their bafenefs,
and the fear of falling into the
hands of the *Medes*, pull'd up their
Coats, and asked them if they had
a mind to take fhelter in the places from whence they came? which
reproach had fo much power over
them, that returning to the fight
again, animated by defpair, and
reincountring their Enemies; they
not only ftopt their Carrier, but
alfo kill'd fo great a number of
them, that they remained mafters
of the Field.

Scipio furnamed *Affricanus*, gained
alfo a Victory over *Antiochus*, King
of *Syria*, by commanding a Legion
which had turned its back in the
beginning of the fight to be put to
the Sword; but this Legion feeing
that they could never expect to
appear any more after this infamy,
behaved themfelves fo bravely afterwards, that they alone were
more

more inftrumental in gaining that
Battel, than all the reft of the Forces which *Scipio* had with him in
the Army ; but there are many
times occafions wherein thefe arts
will not prevail, and where the
Soldiers fear is not to be overcome
either by threats or reproaches; a
Man ought therefore that he may
have no fhare with them in their
infamy in fuch a cafe, chufe rather
to be taken Prifoner.

An Officer ought to be fure to
take care in the day of Battel to
be well Mounted, but he ought to
take greateft care his Horfe be not
hard mouthed. Firft without this,
he cannot be mafter of him, and 'tis
to have too much bufinefs upon ones
hands, to be forc'd to encounter
at the fame time the tricks of a
Horfe and the Enemies charge, and
befides, his Horfe may run away
with him into their Squadrons ; a
Man's honour oftentimes depends
alfo

also upon his Horfe, for if he be
unruly, and bends towards his own
Army, what will hinder thofe that
are apt to cenfure, to attribute fuch
an accident to the Cowardice of
the Rider; for it will not be known
to every body, that he rode upon
an unruly Horfe, and others will
not believe it; the not having
taken care of this, coft *Landreffe*,
Major of the Regiment *de la Chan*,
his Life; for his Horfe being very
hard mouthed, and having followed
a run-away in the Fight, againft
the will of his Rider; he faw himfelf fo defpifed for it by the whole
Army, that he was forc'd in the
next Action that hapned, to expofe
himfelf more than ordinary, to repair the lofs he had fuffered in his
Reputation; but he was not fo
happy as to efcape; and that which
is moft unfortunate in this fort of
difgrace, is, that a Man is not fure
even with the price of his Life to

re-

retrieve his Reputation, some attributing his Resolution to despair, and others explaining it more to his disadvantage.

One must also not affect in the day of Battel, to Ride the fleetest of our Horses; for there being many who please themselves with construing all things maliciously; would publish it, that we have taken it, that we may make the more haft in running away; it being prudence in us to avoid giving any manner of suspicion as much as we can. I approve extreamly of what *Spartacus*, that famous slave did upon this occasion, who being condemned to be a Gladiator, armed himself with Spits, and the first Arms he could find to avoid this infamy, and who became afterwards General of the Army: for being to give Battel to *Crassus*, to shew that he relyed upon nothing but his own Courage,

he

he before the Fight, with his own hand kill'd his Horse, telling those who demanded of him the reason, that if he won the Battel, he should not want a Horse, and that if he loft it, he should have no occasion for one; and indeed these are the thoughts of a brave Man; for to think of escaping, before the Fight is begun, is to shew a meanness of Spirit, and to deserve the scorn of all the World. I do not forbid the using of a Fleet horse in a Fight, but only the doing of it particularly upon that occasion; for why should a Man be hindered from Riding a Horse, which he is used to do at other times? and may he not have use for such a Horse, as well to pursue the Enemies as to fly from them? and why must the intentions of a Man be construed in the worst sense, when he gives no reason for it himself.

The

The King having obferved for fome years, that he loft many Officers for want of their wearing Armor, has made an order, that no Officer fhall go into the Battel without, and that they fhall wear it at all reviews; and fince I have feen fome who out of an exceffive rafhnefs affected to wear none, it is not amifs here to obferve that as it is the mark of extream fear, to wear Armor when others do not; fo it is of extream folly not to wear it when every body elfe does. Firft, they are far from gaining as they think a greater Reputation by it; and they pafs in the opinion of Men of fenfe, for Men of great extravagancy; for if it be true, that a Man is obliged to preferve his riches, to pafs for a wife Man; how much more care ought he to take of his Life, fince that is more valuable to him than all the riches in the World. Secondly, the expofing a Man's felf

M   with-

without neceſſity does not ſhew a true Valour, but a monſtrous Fool-hardineſs, for as every one knowes Valour is the effect of Wiſdom, but Fool-hardineſs the effect of bruitiſhneſs, ſo a Man muſt be more a bruit than all the beaſts together, to affect expoſing himſelf to evident deſtruction when he has the means offered him to defend himſelf; the reaſon which many give for this humour, is that many are kill'd with their **Arms** upon them, as if they had none; but beſides, that this is to intro-duce predeſtinattion which is an opinion I cannot agree to, it is falſe in this particular, for nothing is more common than to hear that ſuch a great Officer had been kill'd but for his Head piece, and that another received ſo many ſhot in his Arms. I eaſily agree with them that things ſo extraordinary often happen, and that Heaven it ſelf ſeems

by

by them to mock at all our endeavours of prevention. Monsieur *de Cavois* Lieutenant in the Guards, elder Brother to the present Quarter-Master-General of the Kings Guards, was kill'd at the Siege of *Lisle*, by a Bullet which entered between his Helmet and Breastpiece, where there seemed to be hardly room for the Bullet to pass. *Godony*, an Officer in the same Regiment died also of a wound he received in the Head, he lifting up his Head-piece to give himself a little air; but what does all this conclude against what I formerly urged? but rather confirms it, for had it not been for the space between the Head-piece and the Breast *Cavois* would not have been kill'd; and *Godony* would have been alive, if he had not put up his Head-piece to give himself air.

M 2 An

An Officer always ought to wear a Coat over his Armor, that the Enemy not knowing he is armed, may in the heat of the Fight spend many of his blows upon him in vain, he ought not to stir from his Troop, but keep the crupper of his Horse in the first Rank; keeping also his Ranks so firmly linked together, that they may not possibly be broken, it being the strength of a Squadron, or a Battalian to be so lockt together. At the Battel of *Rockray*, the Battalian of the Count *de Founteines*, for this reason could not be broken, the Enemy being forc'd to have recourse to their Cannon to do it; when a Troop pursues the Enemy, they are to march as much as they can in Battalia, when they march to a Lane, they must take care to form their Squadron or Battalian so soon as they are past it. A Squadron or a Battalian is most commonly

formed

formed by Files, but when one is
near the Enemy, the beft is to
form it by Ranks; the reafon is,
becaufe a Rank is much more able
to refift than a File, and whilft
that makes good its ground, the
other Ranks have time to form
themfelves behind them; this is
the way ufed in all Fights by
thofe who are moft knowing in
the profeffion, in places where
there are hedges and inclofures,
an Officer of Horfe ought to take
care not to be too far from the Foot,
for if he had not them near him,
the Enemies Foot would do him
no fmall prejudice; wherefore there
is always placed fome few Foot
between the Squadrons, and for
having failed in this, was imputed
to Monfieur *le Brett* all the diforder that hapned in the Battel of
St. *John de Pages*, amongft the Kings
Guards when they come to a hol-
low way, they throw themfelves

M 3   into

into it pell-mell, and soon fall into
their places again; but this ought
not to be an Example for others,
who not having so much experience
will find it hard to fall into their
places again; that which is to be
done in this case is, that every
Right-hand Man of a Rank should
lead his own Rank, and bring it
up into its own place, not troubling
himself with any other; to make
them all keep a true distance, an
Officer ought to put himself at the
head of every Rank, it being easie
for him to recover his **own Post**;
this way will gain a great deal of
time, and things will be done without confusion; when the Enemies
are beaten, and that they fly with
all hast, the Men one Commands
must not be suffered to Plunder,
for that gives time to the Enemy
to get ground, and to gain some
place of safety: for a Man who
is concerned in honour 'for the
service

fervice of the King, ought only to confider the good of the State, which without difpute does not confift in the booty which the Soldiers unfeafonably gain, but in the entire defeat of the Enemies; there is a time for all things, and certainly that is not for pillaging when the Enemy is yet before us; there happen from this many inconveniences, for when the Soldiers are thus fcattered about, what hinders the Enemy from rallying and totally changing the face of affairs? befides, what fecurity have we that their flight is not a Stratagem of War to obtain the Victory by? how many have abandon'd their Carriages and Equipages to amufe the Enemies, and then faln upon them when they thought they were at a great diftance from them? *Cyrus* ufed this artifice in overcoming the *Scythians*; for pretending to be very much amazed with their way

M 4   of

of fighting, and even to be in fear of their strength; he abandon'd his Camp, which was fill'd with all forts of good Wines, at the firft news of their approaching, and whilft they were filling themfelves with them, he fell in upon them, and entirely defeated them. Every one has a knowledge of thefe forts of artifices; but yet he who has ufed them many times cannot defend himfelf from them, fo true it is that Man blinds himfelf in his profperity: The fame *Cyrus*, of whom I have fpoken, gives us a remarkable Example of this; for he who had fo lately catcht the *Scythians*, was caught by them when he fufpected it leaft. He had in the fight kill'd the Son of *Thomyris*, a Princefs who then Reigned over the *Scythians*, who being at the head of the Army her felf, made it appear that there was little difference between her, and a great

Ge-

General : This Queen lov'd her
Son without meafure , and having nothing but revenge in her
thoughts , fled before *Cyrus* to
draw him into fome narrow paf-
fages wherein fhe might fight him
with greateft advantage to her own
fide ; *Cyrus* being flufhed with fuccefs, fet himfelf to purfue her without delay, but not fufpecting her
defign, and engaging himfelf imprudently in a narrow pafs, where
none but the front of his Army
could Fight , *Thomyris* charged
him with fo much fury, that after having kill'd 200000 Men upon the place, took him Prifoner ;
but fhe breathing nothing but revenge, commanded the Throats
to be cut of many of thofe taken
with him, and filling a Tub with
their blood, fhe caufed the Head
of this unfortunate Prince which
fhe had caufed to be cut off , to be
caft into it; reproaching him, that

M 5   fince

since he had been so greedy of human blood in his Life-time, he should have wherewith to glut himself after he was dead. This Example of *Cyrus* shews that it is very difficult to escape Ambuscades when they are cuningly laid: This puts me in mind of what heretofore hapned to the Inhabitants of *Megara*, who themselves were taken Prisoners, when they thought to have made others so ; they had War against the *Athenians*, and knowing that the Ladies of *Athens* were to assemble themselves upon a certain day at a sacrifice, they set sail with a design to surprize them, when they were all assembled in the Temple; but *Pisistrates* an *Athenian* General having notice of it, lay in wait for them upon the *Avenues*, and having given them Battel, he gained the Victory ; after which he went aboard their Ship which he had taken, and placing
some

fome Women upon the deck he
failed for *Megara* ; the Inhabitants
were upon the Rampires waiting
for their Companions, not doubt-
ing at all of the happy fuccefs of
their enterprife, and continuing
ftill to be deceived by the fight of
thefe Women, which they took at
firft for the Prifoners, they came
out to meet them, to lead them in
Triumph ; but the *Athenians* at
the fame moment leaping afhore,
accomplifh'd their fhame by their
defeat, very few having time to
Retreat into the Town. *Sertorius*
by a like Stratagem beat the *Ge-
rifonians*, for after they had failed
of their attempt upon *Caftulo*, a
fmall Town in *Spain* ; he cloathed
his Men with the Cloaths of thofe
he had made Prifoners, advancing
towards their City ; by their refem-
blance he drew out a great many who
ventured without their Walls, fo that
he made a great flaughter of them.

But

But to finish this digreſſion, I ſhall only ſay that it is not only of great conſequence to hinder the Soldiers from ſtragling from their Ranks, for the reaſons I have before mentioned, but alſo if an Officer ſuffers it, he will at laſt be left by himſelf; there are Rules for Plunder, as well as for every thing elſe, there being commonly a party of commanded Men detach'd for that purpoſe, whilſt the reſt make head againſt the Enemy. There is only patience required in this caſe, but the eagerneſs and coveteouſneſs of the Soldiers, is ſuch, that unleſs the Officer has a careful Eye upon them, they ſeldom have ſo much patience; by theſe means an Army puts it ſelf out of danger of receiving an affront, for whilſt they are Plundering, if the Enemy make any attempt, thoſe who are at their Arms receive them, and give time to the Pillagers to draw themſelves

to-

together, the Pillagers themselves
not loosing their booty, they delivering it to be kept by some amongst
them, till the Enemy be beaten
back; the same way ought to be
used in relation to the Prisoners
which are made in the Fight, that is
to put them into the hands of some
detach'd for that purpose, they
never fail in this Article, but the
other is far more difficult to be
observed, because of the coveteous-
ness of the Soldiers, which is sometimes so great, that they harken
not to any word of Command; at
such a time an Officer must use all
manner of means, and even kill
one amongst them to make the
rest return to their Duty; for altho I have said in the former Chapter that mildness is preferrable
to severity, yet there are times
when the first would be extremely
hurtful; besides the Soldiers esteem
an Officer but the more for it,
                                    being

being satisfied when they calmly consider it, that in such a case he had reason to do what he did, and that it was they who forc'd him to it.

CHAP. XVII.

That an Officer ought to understand his Duty in a Garison, as well as in the Army.

WHen a Campaign is ended, the Forces are sent into Winter-Quarters; some remaining in the frontier places, others being sent home into their own Countries to be in Garison. These last seem to have some advantage over the others, because having nothing to do, they have time to recover themselves; whereas those which remain in the frontier Towns continue to wear themselves out, being

ing all the Winter obliged to be
upon Duty, they sometimes being sent out upon Parties, sometimes upon Convoys, and sometimes for Escorts. Those who are
upon the frontiers have this advantage, that they learn their
Trade much better than the others,
because there always falls out
there, something new, by which
an Officer may learn. This is of
use to him upon many occasions,
because when there happens any
difficulty he is thereby much the readier to resolve it in himself, having
seen the same thing happen before
and decided ; and there happens
sometimes such things as are not to
be seen elsewhere, one of which I shall
here relate, which divided the judgments of many of the profession,
being in Garison at *Owdenard*,
there hapned a dispute for Command, which appeared to be very
difficult to judge, altho the Kings
re-

regulations which seem to have provided for every thing were consulted; it was concerning a certain Party which was commanded out, and which consisted of almost all the Horse of the Garison, when they were drawn up in the Parade place; the first thing considered was to decide to whom the Command did belong, there being only Captains upon the place, all the Colonels being absent; at last it was agreed upon, that it belonged to the Marquess of *Ailli*, a Captain in the Regiment of *Genlis*, but his Lieutenant whose Name was *Legrand*, and who had not yet said any thing, began to dispute the Command with him; saying, that having been a Captain before the *Pyranean* treaty, and it being ordain'd in a certain Article of the Kings orders, that one who had been a Captain, should retake the Rank of his Commission in a detachment

tachment, he claimed it as his right
to retake his, which was to Command the party preferrably to all
of them; every one looked upon
this pretenfion to be very ftrange,
efpecially of a Lieutenant, in relation to his Captain, but when the
Kings orders were examined, no
body durft decide it of his own
head, and they were forc'd to defire Monfieur *de Rochpert*, Governor of the place, to give his judgment in it; who having read over
feveral times the Kings orders, af-
ked the opinion of the principal
Officers of the Garifon, who being
inclined to take part with the Captains, decided the thing in favour
of the Marquefs *Dailli*, which he
the next day conformed himfelf to;
Legrand was to wait upon him,
and without failing in the refpect
he owed to him, defired him to
let him know upon what grounds
he had given judgment againft him,
which

which Monfieur *de Rochpert* was willing to do; telling him, that that ordinance was to be underftood only concerning Captains, and not concerning inferior Officers; but *Legrand* anfwer'd him, that then this Article was needlefs, for that always the eldeft Captains Commanded the others; Monfieur *de Rochpert* anfwer'd, that he agreed fo far with him, but that the precedency of the Regiments being according to their Incorporation, and not their Antiquity; this was what this ordinance had provided for explaining it, that the eldeft Captain being the laft in the body, fhould Command thofe who were before him in a Regiment, if they met upon a detachment; this was the Colour that Monfieur *de Rochpert* pretended he had for the judgment he had given; but many were of opinion, that he had done an injuftice to *Legrand*, and that the

Article

Article was to be obferved literally, and to fhew the reafon they had for alledging what they did, they faid, that it was no new thing to fee an Officer fometimes of lefs quality than the other Command him; they inftanced *Reveillon* who was then Lieutenant Colonel of the Regiment of *Anion* , whom Monfieur *de* St. *Geran* Colonel of that Regiment, had for a long time obey'd, and *Montaigle* a Captain in the Royal foreign Regiment , who at this prefent, Commands the Count *de Coigni* who is Colonel of it ; and many others , who for brevity fake I fhall omit, concluding from thence , that *Legrand* might as well Command the Marquefs *D'Ailli* , as *Reveillion* the Count *de* St. *Geron*, and *Montaigle* the Count *de Caigni* ; but without pretending to determine , I fhall only anfwer the objections that may be made to me ; and fay, that

when

when Monfieur *de Reveillon* Commanded Monfieur St. *Geron*, it was becaufe he was a Brigadier, and Monfieur *de* St. *Geron* was not, as alfo that when Monfieur *de Coigni* obey'd *Montaigle*, it was becaufe *Montaigle* had a Commiffion of Colonel, altho he had but a Company ; and which was more antient than that of Monfieur *Coigni* ; and fince I have now fpoken of St. *Geron*, *Coigni* and *Montaigle*, I think it will not be amifs, to fhew here in what a Lieutenant Colonel who is a Brigadier, commands his Colonel, and in what his Colonel commands him. The Colonel obeys him in every thing, except in what concerns the particular management of his Regiment, and has alfo the fame authority over the Lieutenant Colonels Company, as if the Lieutenant Colonel were not a Brigadier: As to a Captain of Horfe who has a Commiffion of Co-

Colonel, and whose Commiffion is
more antient than that of his Colonel, he always obeys his Colonel,
excepting in a detachment; for
whether in Fight or in a March,
the Colonel is always at the head
of the firft Squadron, and leaves
him the fecond to Command; in
the Horfe there are fome of thefe
Captains who have Colonels Commiffion, but this is almoft all
that they can pretend to, when
they have no Regiment which goes
under their name, never having
feen, as I remember any but the
Chevalier *de Efclainvilliers*, come
to be a Brigadier without having
one; it is not the fame in the Foot,
where the Lieutenant Colonels are
every day made Brigadiers, altho
they have no Regiment of their
own; the reafon in my opinion is,
that there being fewer Regiments
of Foot, than of Horfe, and that
they alfo feeming to be referved for
Men

Men of the greatest quality, it is not just that a Man of desert, because he is not rich must bound his Fortune with a small Command; besides a Man must have a great Estate to be a Colonel of Foot; for unless he know himself to be in a condition to maintain a great port, I would never advise a Man to take such a Command: for it is quite another thing to be a Colonel of Foot, than of Horse; yet the Colonels of Foot, as well as those of Horse, are much fallen from what they were heretofore; for before the *Pyrenean* peace, they disposed of all the Commissions in the Regiments, the Court always gratifying the Persons named by them, without ever refusing it; but altho that might have given them a great power, yet they had that amongst the Officers of the Regiment but according to their Courage; for the

the cuftom of thofe times was, that a Colonel was forc'd to fight five or fix Captains before he could be confidered by the others. This was practifed, efpecially in the Old Regiments, and principally in thofe of them which were fmall ones, wherein there were Captains who would take upon them, as much as if they were Generals of an Army: *Arbonville*, a Gentleman of the Province of *Normandy*, who had been bred up Page to the King, ufed in that time a Radomontade, which did not fucceed well with him; for having bought the Command of one of thefe little Old Regiments, when he came to be receiv'd, he declared at the head of the Regiment, that he had brought with him twelve Swords of the fame length to try them with the moft mutinous; and that if there were any one of them, who was not fatisfied with his being Colonel,

he

he defired to let him know it, and
he would foon give him fatisfaction.
The next day all the Captains of
his Regiment came to him, and
each defired a Sword; but it not
being poffible for him to fight with
them all at once, he agreed with
the Captain who paffed for the
boldeft amongft them, to fight
with him firft; thinking that if
he would mafter him, he fhould
ftrike a terror into all the reft;
but, the fortune of Arms being
againft him; he took another
to task, by whom he was alfo
beaten, and was fo by five or fix,
one after another : the Captains do
at this time fhew themfelves much
wifer, and none of them dare draw
their Sword againft their Colonel,
for if they fhould, an exemplary
punifhment would be inflicted upon them for it; yet if a Colonel
be not in efteem with his Regiment, the Captains find out other
ways

ways to get him removed, in which they sometimes succeed; in the year 1675. the Regiment of *Langudock* deputed some of their number to the King, to desire that their Colonel might be removed, and prevailed so much by their sollicitations, that the King granted their request. In the Horse the factions are seldom known, but sometimes there are secret ones; of which the Majors make themselves heads: a prudent Man therefore must endeavour to live well with them; but if you be forc'd to take part with any, let him stick to a Colonel, for after all, there is nothing better than holding by the body of the Tree; that is to say, to have no other interest, than that of ones Chief.

But I am come too far from the subject which I proposed to my self in this Chapter, which was to shew that an Officer ought to

N   know

know as well what is his Duty
in a Garifon, as when he is in
the Army. There are two forts
of Garifons, the one upon the
Frontier, and the other in the
Heart of the Country: Although
the laft feems not to require much
experience, yet there happens in
them many times fuch accidents
that he would pafs his time very ill,
if he where wholly to feek in
them. I fhall relate fome Examples to juftifie this, after I have
faid a word of what paffes in Frontier places; the fame Duty is done
in Frontier places, as in the Army,
excepting that the Orders are not
always given by the fame Perfon.
I have already fpoken amply of
this, and therefore it will be
fuperfluous to repeat the fame
thing over again; every one is
detach'd in his turn, whether for
the Guard or for Parties, and every
Night they fend out a Patrole.
It

It is not in thefe Garifons where one has much trouble, for one does not fear the Enemy, or at leaft if one does, all the care lies upon the Governor; and in obeying him, and doing ones Duty, a Man is free from all anxiety and care; if there happens an alarm, the Foot run to the Rampart, and the Horfe to the Parade place, or draw to the efplanade, after having received the Town-Majors Orders fo to do; for till then they are only to draw up, and to be ready to March at the firft word of Command. When Troops are fent into Villages or Caftles, whofe fituation is fo advantageous, that it is neceffary to keep them, an Officer muft neceffarily know how to behave himfelf in this fervice, there being none to advife with: if it be in a Village that you are pofted, you muft immediately ftop all the Avenues, and retire

into

into the Church if there be one,
or into some house which may be
defended; both Night and Day
there must be a Guard set at the
end of the Village, unless the passage may be cut; in such a case
it may be enough to place one at
the first Barracado ; this Guard
must be often visited, and especially in the Night, for then most
commonly the Enemy makes his
attempt, there are often Orders
given to have an Advanced-guard
in the Day-time, at about five or
six hundred paces from the Village or Castle, as the ground is
more or less divided by hedges
and ditches ; but there must be
great care taken not to set them,
till the place has been viewed by
the Patrole, which is a detachment from the Guard which is to
be set; which during this time,
as well as all the rest of the Garison are at their Arms, till the
Pa-

Patrole be returned ; the Garifon then advances to a certain place where they are drawn up in Battalia, fo that there remains in the Church or in the Caftle, only fuch as are upon the Guard, who are likewife at their Arms till the Garifon are re-enter'd, which they never do, till the Guard they went to relieve be returned; thefe Advanc'd-guards return always at Sun fet, and the Guard of the Caftle or of the Church, always are at their Arms; when they fee them coming; there is lefs to be feared in thefe places, than in walled Towns that are weak, becaufe the circumvallation being much lefs, the Enemy is feldom to be feared but on one fide, fo that if there be a good Guard placed on that fide ; it puts the Garifon out of danger of any attempt; in thefe weak Towns one muft have a Retreat ready, in

cafe

cafe of furprize, either in the Church or in fome ftrong Houfe, and place Men round about them, that if the Enemy fhould Scale the Walls, they may hold out for fome time, and make fome Compofition; *Montgomery*, who was a Captain of Horfe, and a near Kinfman of the Marquefs I formerly fpoke of, was for not having ufed this caution, with his whole Troop of Horfe furprized in a little Town in *Alfatia*, and carried away Prifoners; he was kill'd fince, fo there can be no great prejudice to inftance him for an Example.

I forgot to mention that there muft always be in thefe forts of Garifons, a Centry or two placed in the Steeple, two being beft; for they being allowed to talke together in fuch a Poft, there will be the lefs danger of their fleeping; this is what is to be faid in grofs,

grofs, concerning Frontier Garifons, for I will not here fpeak of
the Signal which is to be given for
the demanding of Succours, in cafe
of need; for that depends upon
the nearnefs of Quarters, and the
Orders we receive, an Officer not
daring of his own head to
quit his Garifon, upon any accompt whatfoever; as for inland
Garifons, I have many things to
fay of them, although they feem,
as I have faid, not to require
any great experience; yet one
muft have more than one thinks
of, there happening every day
differences between the Officers and the Inhabitants, the
Officers expecting to have the
Kings Orders literally obferved;
and the others explaining them
according to their own humors,
or rather intereft. There are two
forts of orders, the one to pay to
content, and the other wherein

N 4   no

no mention is made of any payment : The firſt is that which caufes moſt difputes between the Officer and the Inhabitant, becaufe neither of them underſtand it, or at leaſt pretend they do not: I have known the Inhabitants upon ſuch an Order, pretend that the Soldiers are to pay the fame with other Men; and the Officers to the contrary, alledge that they are not obliged to any payment; in both which they willfully miſtake; the Kings intentions being, when he gives thefe Orders; being that the Inhabitant ſhould get nothing by the Soldier, and that the Soldier ſhould make the Inhabitant lofe nothing by him; that is to fay, that the Soldier is to pay his Landlord for his provifion, what it is fold for in grofs in the Market, and not as it is fold in Retail; I know very well that a

great

great many Officers pretend that, this Order is not to be explained in this manner, but so much the worse for them if they explain it otherwise, for they ought to follow the intention of the Kings Orders, and not exact any thing beyond it; wherefore an Officer muſt take great care in this caſe, that his Soldiers live frugally, and that the Inhabitants do not give them all they ask for; for they having but a little Money to ſpend, they are to be treated according to their Purſe, and not their Appetite. The Inhabitants cannot refuſe advancing proviſion for a Man and Horſe for Ten days; at the end of which time, they may demand payment for it; but if the Officer have not received pay for his Soldiers, they muſt continue to furniſh them until they can receive Money. The Forces are at preſent ſo very

N 5   well

well paid, that this feems to be a needlefs remark; yet it being poffible that fuch a thing may happen, and which has not been is not Example, I fhall here fet down what is to be done upon this occafion; as alfo, how an Officer is to behave himfelf when he receives Orders to remove to other Quarters, and has not Money to difcharge thofe which he leaves; he muft then give his Note for it, and they cannot refufe it, and much lefs ftop him, unlefs they have a mind to bring themfelves into trouble enough; all that they can do for their own fafety, is to put a ftop upon the Companies pay in the hands of the Paymafter, that being as good as ready Money to them, there being fo good an Order now eftablifhed, that none have reafon to complain.

There

There are places where the Inhabitants do not know what belongs to Soldiers, not having had many Garisons amongst them; so that they think if they have the strength on their side, they may force the Soldiery to what they please; I pitty these sort of People, for without doubt they will soon find cause to repent this humor; for an Officer who understands himself, cares not whether he be strong or weak, to have that allowed him which is due to him; for having Justice of his side, he knows that the King will be sure to do him Justice upon the Inhabitants who refuse it. A certain Author gives us an authentical instance of this; his relation is this, that the *Chevallier* Duke, having orders to have his Winter-quarters in *Mazeares*, retired to two Country houses near the Town, upon the

re-

refusal which the Inhabitants made to him of furnishing him with Forage, according to the Kings Orders, where he lived upon the Provisions which were in the two houses, till an Officer which he had sent to Court to complain, had brought him the Kings Orders for what he was to do; which was to return to *Mazeares*, and to Quarter upon them at discretion for some time; upon these occasions, an Officer needs only to write to the Secretary of War, for he never fails to inform the King of it, and the Troops lose nothing for having been ill used; but it is not enough to send up to him barely a Letter only, but must accompany it with an information signed by all the Officers; and wherein the fact is recited in short. A Captain of Horse, who understood his business very well, but
who

who was of a very paffionate humor, having had a Quarter of
Rendezvouz given him at *Tarafcon*
in the County of *Foix*, and de-
fireing rather to have it in
Money, which was allowed of in
that time; he went often thither
to demand his due, but in vain,
all the Inhabitants of the Country
having made a Combination together, by which they obliged themfelves one to the another, not to
pay any towards Quarters of Rendezvouz, fo that the Officers being
out of hopes of getting any Money out of them, fhould not demand it any more in thofe parts;
at length this Officer feeing himfelf forced to take his Quarters
in fpecie, borrowed 50 Horfe-men
to make his Troop the more numerous, which was intended for
pure vexation, (a Troop confift-
ing but of 50 Horfe) and went
to the Town, being accompanied
by

by one of the Governor of the
Province's Guards, to make use
of him as time and place required; he not being able to bear
it, that the other Captains should
get 942 Livers from their Quarters of Rendezvouz, and that he
should get nothing; being come
to *Tarrafcon*, the Confuls delivered out to him Billets for 100
Horfe, in which they shew'd the
little knowledge they had of the
Kings eftablishment, by which a
Troop is to confift but of 50;
yet when they perceived that this
lay very heavy upon their Town,
they two days afterwards thought
of leffening the allowance to one
half, (which was then of three
quarts of Wine, 24 Ounces of
Bread, a Bufhel of Oates and 20
Pound of Hay, *per diem*, all according to the Wait and Meafure
of *Paris*;) faying, that one half of
it was enough for a Horfe, and
Horfe-

Horse-man; the Captain who defired nothing more than a Ca-
vil to have the pretence of re-
venging himfelf, gave the Confuls
very provoking language, who
ftanding much upon their points,
returned it to him, and they
refufing to deliver out any more
provifions than what they had
agreed upon, the Captain col-
lered one of them, and taking
away the Staff which he carried
in his hand as a mark of his
Authority, he broke it about his
Ears, which made the whole
Town rife up in Arms; they
began to ring their Watch-bell
to call to their affiftance, not
only thofe of the out skirts of
the City, but the Inhabitants of
the Mountains which are round
about the Town; the Captain
feeing himfelf in this extremity,
put on refolution, and having
call'd his Men about him, feiz'd
upon

upon the Market-place, making his Men take ftraw in their hands, and threatned to fet the Town on fire if they charged him, ftill taking the Governors Guard for a witnefs of what paffed; fo that the Inhabitants fearing his defperate humor, hindering the Villagers from entring into the Town, Capitulated with him, chufing rather to pay him his Quarter of Rendezvouz, than fuffer things to come to a greater heighth.

There every day happen differences between the Officers, and the Inhabitants; but an Officer is very ftrong when he has juftice on his fide. I have known an Example of this in the fame Country I have now fpoken of; and this Example appears to me, to be more confiderable than the former, for after the fetling of a Garifon, t

feems

feems to me that there ought
not to be allowed any change,
without being refponfible, for the
evil confequences which may happen from it; two Troops having
Orders to remain at *Labaſtide de
feron,* paying the Inhabitants *to
content*; a new Captain commanding the Quarters, eſtabliſhed all
things as well as he underſtood
them; that is to fay, like a Man who
underſtood not his buſineſs in the
leaſt; foon after, the other Captain coming, and being furprized
at what his Comrade had done;
demanded to make a new agreement with the Inhabitants, and
they refolving to ſtand to the a-
greement made with the other Captain, there arofe a hot difpute,
upon which the Inhabitants pub-
liſhed an order of Common-Coun-
cil, to forbid furniſhing any thing
more to either Troop. The
Captain furprifed with their way
of

of proceeding, and knowing himself to be in the right, commanded the Men to take Provision and Forage from them by force, if they would not give it them willingly, which Command soon proved the occasion of their coming to blows on both sides; but besides that the Inhabitants were beaten, they were also punished for it by the Court, for they had more Troops sent, who made an end to eat them up; the other Order wherein there is no mention of paying *to content*, does also sometimes cause quarrels, and that because the Officers will always find their accompt, and in truth the Inhabitants are to find Lodging and the Utensils, *viz.* Fire and Candle, *&c.* but there are sometimes secret orders sent, to the Intendants of the Provinces to see that the Forces be well used; this is done
especially

especially after any long Campaign, where the Soldier has endured much fatigue; wherefore the Inhabitants ought never to be stiff in requiring the Execution of the King's Orders according to the letter, till they have first advised with the Intendant; how they are to behave themselves, these secret orders were very often sent when the King gave nothing for the Utensils, for the Captains not being able to recruit their Troops without help it was necessary to allow them some way or other to enable themselves to compleat them: but since the King has furnished this out of his own Coffers, there has been care taken to keep the Troops within the bounds of their Duty, and whoever dares offend is soon punished, neither quality nor service exempting them from punishment

if

if they deserve it. I have known a Son of a Marshal *de France* sent to the *Bastille*, upon a complaint made of him by the Inhabitants of his Quarters: so that if some Inhabitants have Quartered whole Regiments, without receiving payment for them, it may be said it was because they were willing to do it, or that they rather chuse thus to buy their peace by sacrificing something, than to claim what is due to them, and live in Combustion; for it must be agreed, that Soldiers are never in a good humor, when their Landlord does not give them some small gratification; there are two sorts of Utensil, that which the King gives which is taken in Money, and the other due from the Inhabitants which is given in kind, the which they are not to turn into Money upon any pretence whatsoever; as to the first, which

which is defigned for the recruiting of the Troops; the King orders fome of it to be given to the common Soldiers, but a Captain who knows his profeffion is not fo fimple as to truft them with it; the reafon is, that if they did not employ this Money in buying of Stockins, Shooes and Linnen for them, for which this is defign'd, the Captain would be obliged to buy all thefe things himfelf, for it would be fo much lofs to him to relie upon their honefty, for a Commiffary of Mufter feldom troubles himfelf to know what they have receiv'd, but only to fee them in a condition of marching and doing their Duty; a Captain ought therefore to know, that the Utenfil that the King gives is defign'd for two things, *viz.* to buy Horfes for the Troop, and
pro-

provide Cloaths for the Soldiers; the Money for the Horses is to be taken out of that part of the Utensil, for which the Captain is to give account to no body; the Money for the Cloaths is to be taken out of the rest of this Utensil, and this belongs to the private Soldiers; so that an Officer is obliged to be accomptable to them for it before he goes into the Field, or as soon as he comes there. The Troopers pretended when the King gave this allowance first, that they were to have it without deduction, and that the Captains were to Cloath them, but the Commissaries who were deputed to judge between them, decided this point otherwise; and that further, it was lawful for the Captains to stop some of their pay, if the Utensil was not sufficient to do it, which happens but too often, Twelve Crowns and

and a half, which they get out
of a Winter-Quarters, not being
enough to put them in Equipage;
it is the same with the Foot, in
which the Soldiers receive nothing
till they are Cloathed from head
to foot, and that is what makes
the Forces appear so well in Cloaths
at this time; a Captain chusing
rather to lay out the last penny
upon their Cloaths, than let them
have it to increase their debauchery; and besides this uses the
Soldiers to have a care of their
Cloaths, for knowing that what
others are bought for them, must
be at their own expence, they
endeavour to preserve those they
have. I have said before, that an
Officer owed an account to his Men
when they came out of their
Winter Quarters, and this is so
true, that I have known a Captain of Horse suspended for having
refused to give it to a private
Cen-

Centry of his Troop; wherefore an Officer ought always to keep his Book of Accompts in order and to shew it the Soldiers, it being best for him to Accompt with them of himself, before they require it of him; for it is certain, that if he be indebted to some a small matter, others will prove to be more indebted to him; and if he did not reckon with these last, and make up a state of the Accompt in their presence, they will not remember it the next year, or at leastwise pretend they do not.

CHAP.

C H A P. XVIII.

Of the Authority of the Commissa-
ries over the Forces.

THe Office of the Com-
missary is not only to
Muster the Forces, but the Commissaries also take Cognizance of
their Quarters, Forages, and of
all disorders which happen in
their March ; but notwithstanding their power, an Officer who
intends to do his Duty as he
ought, is not to apply himself
to make Court to them, there
being none but those who en-
deavor to make unlawful advantages who have need to do it ;
but he ought not on the contrary to be wanting in civility
to them, but shew a respect for

O   them;

them; the King having chosen
them to fee that every one
acquit himfelf of his Duty, it
would be to fhew very little
fubmiffion to the orders of his
Prince, to defpife thofe whom
he honours with his choice; he
ought not therefore to make any
reflection upon their Birth, which
would often incline us to make
little Accompt of them, but upon their Character which requires
us to have fome confideration
for them. An Officer of Quality
asked one of them as he was
Muftering his Regiment, which
weighed moft in his Pockets,
his Mufter-Rolls or his Mafters
Prayer Books, for it was faid the
Commiffary had been a Foot-
man: in my opinion thefe are
unfeafonable railleries; and if
this Officer will fpeak the truth,
he muft confefs he was difpleafed

with

with this Officer upon some other account, but whether for his too great severity in his Mustering of his Troop, or for any other reason I will not determine; the Officers are to have a respect for the Commissaries, much more ought the Commissares to have so for the Officers; for they ought not to take upon them, because they have a power of obliging them; for they cannot do a pleasure to any body without being guilty of a breach of their own Duty, for which their Lives are answerable; but as there are many of these who forget themselves so much, as to think themselves much greater than they are; so I must confess, there are many Officers who use them so ill, that they bring themselves into great trouble for it. I have seen many Exam-

ples

ples of this kind, of which I shall relate those which I can remember; after which, I shall shew what power they have which cannot be disputed with them. St. *Simon*, a Colonel of Horse of whom I formerly spoke, being in Garison at *Ath*, and going to the Magazine of Hay, upon the complaint which his Regiment had made to him, that the Hay was not good, struck the Store-keeper several blows with his Cane, which occasioned some disturbance; and immediately a Commissary call'd *du Chaunoi*, came up, and having checkt St. *Simon* for his passion; St. *Simon* answered him, that Thieves always took part with their fellows, and therefore he did not wonder that he took the Store-keepers part; *du Chaunoi* was concerned at these words; and

and faying, he would write word
of it to Monfieur *de Loueru*; St.
Simon continued his abufes, and
was lifting up his hand to ftrike
at him, which forc'd *du Chaunoi*
to go home, whither he was no
fooner come, but he wrote word
of it to Monfieur *de Louois*,
who not approving of thefe pro-
ceedings; fent order that St. *Simon* fhould keep Prifon for a
Fortnight; after which, the Governor of the place was enjoin-
ed to affemble all the chief
Officers of the Garifon together,
before whom St. *Simon* was ordered to ask pardon of the
Commiffary; this was fet down
in exprefs terms in the order, and
St. *Simon* notwithftanding his
high Spirit was forc'd to obey:
one cannot take too much care
to avoid having any difpute with
thofe fort of People; for if a

O 3 Man

Man defpifes them, he is forc'd
afterwards to fhew them a refpect, and fometimes worfe happens : and I have feen Officers of
great defert and long fervice in
danger of being cafhier'd, for
having ufed them otherwife than
he ought to have done. St. *Andre* a Brigadier of Foot, and
Lieutenant Colonel of the Regiment of *Saux* and a Man of Courage, but whofe paffion had very much prejudiced him in the
making of his Fortune, cudgel'd
a Commiffary, becaufe having
feen him at *Perpinian*, he did notwithftanding go and Mufter his
Regiment that was Quarter'd
thereabout, without giving him
notice of it: St. *Andre* was fufpended for this, and if he had
not had a great many Friends
who begg'd for him, and pleaded his long fervice, he had
been

been cashier'd without mercy;
there is nothing so dangerous as
this sort of violence, Wise men
abstain from using it, not only
towards the Comissaries, but
towards the meanest Persons whatsoever. The Marshal *de la Ferte*,
who was always of an imperious
humor, once acknowledged this
fault in himself very gentelely; he
then commanded the Kings Army
jointly with Monsieur *de Turene*,
so that there being some jealousie
between them, he hapned one
day to strike one of the Guards
of that Prince, whether to discharge his Choller, or finding
him in a fault I cannot tell:
the Guard immediately went to
his Master, exaggerating to him
this Action of the Marshal,
to inspire him with the thoughts
of taking revenge upon him; but
Monsieur *Turene* far from entring

into any paffion; told him, that
certainly he had much provoked
the Marfhal, fince he had ufed
him as he had done; and calling
at the fame time the Captain of
his Guards, he ordered him to
go with him to the Marfhal *la
Farté*, and to put him into his
hands, to difpofe of him as he
pleafed : Monfieur *de la Ferté*,
who expected that this Prince
would have made another fort of
refentment of it, was extremely
furpriz'd with this moderation,
and beginning to reflect upon his
own paffion, confeft openly
to thofe who were with him,
that Monfieur *de Turene* would
always be as wife as he was
mad; he could not in my opinion better fhew the concern he
had for it, and indeed when we
have hapned to do an Action,
that we ought not to have done it,

                              feems

seems to me that there needs no other but our selves to condemn us, if we make the least reflection upon our Actions.

But to come back to the power of the Commissaries, it is certain they have an absolute power over all Quarters of Soldiers, either in relation to the Officers, or to the Mayors and chief Magistrates of the Town. It belongs also to them, to see that the first commit no violences, and that the last be not partial in exempting their Friends and Kindred; as to the first, they may give them Billets to Quarter in the houses of any of the Inhabitants, and these Billets are as good as if they had been given out by the Officers of the Town. The Officers of the Army easily acknowledge their

O 5   power

power in this, but the Officers of the Towns are very unwilling to do it , because it diminishes very much their power, but nothing is more sure than that the Commissaries have this power; and I have seen a thing happen hereupon which shews it plainly, the Regiment of *Alsatia* was there in Garison, and the Officers of the Town having exempted from Quarters the Brother-in-law of an Alderman who was liable to them ; the Commissary sent a Captain to Lodge at his house, and gave him a Billet for the same ; there arose upon this a great contest between the Captain and the Brother-in-law of the Alderman; the Captain endeavouring to Lodge there by force, the other shut the door against him , so that the Captain was going to break it open,

upon

upon which the Neighbours went immediately to give notice to the Officers of the Town of what was doing, who came without delay upon the place, but they inftead of appeafing the Tumult, raifed the People againft the Soldiers, many being wounded on both fides, at length the Soldiers got the maftery; but not being contented with this alone, and expecting a greater fatisfaction, they fent to Court an Information of what had hapned; and the King being informed of it, the Officers of the Town were turned out, and others put in their places. The Cognizance of all abufes committed by Mayors and other chief Officers, in relation to Quarters belongs to the Commiffary alone; as for the Officers of the Army, they ought not to meddle are dishoneft, it is good to know their tricks, to be able to defend our felves from their rapine; it is neceffary therefore that an Officer know, that the Oates which the King orders for their Winter-Quarters, ought to be meafur'd by the meafure of *Paris*, and he ought to fee, if the meafure which is in the Magazine, be the fame with that of that City; if it be not, it is the fault of the Store-keeper or the Commiffary, or fometimes of both together, for the Commiffary having Orders to infpect the behaviour of the Store-keeper, he would never dare to cheat the Officers, if he were not fure of the others fupport: in this cafe an Officer ought to make his complaint to the Commiffary, as if he did not fufpect him to be in Combination with the other, and

and he will be sure to do him
Juftice, not only for the future,
but alfo for the time paft; the
meafures which I have feen in all the
Magazines, either in *Lorrain*, *Alfatia*, or *Catalonia*, are all marked;
as are thofe remaining in the
Manner-houfes of Lords, with
which Tole Corn is meafur'd;
fo that one would think that no
knavery could be ufed, but yet
I have feen Bufhels fo pared at
the top, that they wanted a
great deal of what they fhould
hold; the Store-keeper runs a
great hazard, when he practifes
thefe forts of knavery, for if he be
found out it will coft him his
Life; but a prudent Officer having difcovered any fuch knavery, ought to content himfelf with
punifhing him in the purfe; for
that will help him to make his
Troop better, and his Death will
do

do him no good; it is alfo to be
obferved, that the meafure ought
to be heaped, at leaft the Oates
were always meafured fo in the
laft Winter-Quarters; yet there
have been Commiffaries feen,
who pretending to be ignorant
of the Orders, have made them
be delivered out by a ftricken
meafure, and divided the over-
plufs with the Store-keeper to
his own advantage; this is alfo a
Capital offence, becaufe the Horfes not having all the Oates they
fhould have to recruit themfelves,
it is undoubtedly a great prejudice
to the Kings fervice.

Commiffaries have been alfo
fometimes known to compound
with the Inhabitants for their
Hay, and to deliver that which
was mufty to the Officers; in
this cafe, the Officers ought to be
fevere

severe with them; for altho I said before, that the Commissaries had full power over the Forage, that is only to be understood when they do the King service as they ought, for otherwise we are not to look upon them.

These are the ways the Commissaries make use of to cheat the Officers, as to the Corporations they are often cheated by them also; because they having a dependance upon the Commissaries, by reason of the Winter Quarters, which they are obliged to provide, they dare not complain what reason soever they may have, and it often happens that the Commissaries have Quarters assigned them in every quarter of the Town, but they not being able to make use of above one, convert the others

into

into Money; it is the Kings and the Corporations interest only, which is concern'd fo, that it is their part to look after it; but to fpeak no more of thefe forts of mifdemeanours, I fhall inform you that befides the power that Commiffaries have in relation to Quarters and Forage, they have alfo a gteat deal of Authority given them, in relation to the difputes which fall out between the Soldiers and the Inhabitants, for their Information is always believed preferrably to that of the parties concern'd, fo that which fide foever gains them, is fure to have what he defires: Thus Monfieur *de Vervins* the Commiffary of War, for the Forces which had their Winter-Quarters in the Country of *Foix*, contributed very much towards the command

mand, which the Governor of that Province received, to dispose of his Employment by the frequent complaints he made against him.

It belongs to the Commissaries to Administer the Oath to all the Officers who come into the service; there is due to him for this the Sword which the Officer then wears: but they often wearing one which is not of any great value, this Fee is commonly changed into a present of Money, to the value of a Months pay; there are some Commissaries who pretend that an Officer who is prefer'd, owes them a new present, because he is to take the Oath again; but this is an abuse, and an Officer who knows the Word, will not yield to it, being only due at the first entring into the service.

F I N I S.